AESOP'S FABLES
in the
Executive
Suite

AESOP'S FABLES
in the Executive Suite

John S. Morgan
ILLUSTRATED BY
Larry Sowinski

 Van Nostrand Reinhold Company
New York / Cincinnati / Toronto / London / Melbourne

Van Nostrand Reinhold Company Regional Offices:
New York Cincinnati Chicago Millbrae Dallas

Van Nostrand Reinhold Company International Offices:
London Toronto Melbourne

Copyright © 1974 by Litton Educational Publishing, Inc.

Library of Congress Catalog Card Number: 73-23000
ISBN: 0-442-25516-0

Manufactured in the United States of America

Published by Van Nostrand Reinhold Company
450 West 33rd Street, New York, N.Y. 10001

Published simultaneously in Canada by Van Nostrand Reinhold Ltd.

15 14 13 12 11 10 9 8 7 6 5 4 3 2 1

Library of Congress Cataloging in Publication Data

Morgan, John Smith, 1921–
  Aesop's fables in the executive suite.

  1. Success. I. Aesopus. Fabulae. English.
II. Title.
HF5386.M762   658.4   73-23000
ISBN 0-442-25516-0

To Virginia, of course.

Preface

This book could be subtitled *Fables for Promotion* because it narrates typical situations of today that illustrate lessons for the ambitious who want better jobs in business, industry, government and education.

I use an adaptation of the device of the fable as a method to make a point. Fables go back to the earliest tellers of tales in India and Egypt during the fourteenth century B. C. But a man (or men) called Aesop perfected the genre in ancient Greece. Fables were at first only narrated and thus handed down through the uncertain channel of oral tradition. This accounts for our receiving Aesop's fables in many variations.

Most of Aesop's fables involve animals, although some deal with humans and gods. By clothing men in the guise of animals, the fabulist could lampoon them safely. Undoubtedly, some fables were attacks on dictators or other figures of Aesop's day. He was born about 620 B. C., probably a slave who was freed because of his learning and wit. He ended his days in the service of Croesus of Sardis as a kind of foreign minister or roving ambassador. In that capacity he travelled widely in the world of his time, giving currency to his fables and also observing human nature under many conditions.

I present more than forty of Aesop's fables in the form of the limerick. Socrates put some of Aesop's fables into verse, so the precedent for doing this goes far back. Even the origins of the limerick, while shrouded in mystery, may go back to Aristophanes.

Isaac Bashevis Singer writes: "Aesop's fables teach lessons both in life and literature that are valid today and will remain so forever. Thousands of years ago he pointed out that no change in system can do away with the aggressor, the liar, the flatterer, the intriguer, the exploiter, the parasite."

I say "Amen" and have tried to point out in this book how the knowledge could help you if you seek to advance in your career. My format is to versify the original fable, present Aesop's moral and then give a contemporary illustration from the world of industry, business, government or education, ending with a modern precept for promotion. The fables are arranged in alphabetical order.

If you recognize yourself or others in any of the cases, even though they are fictitious, remember one of Aesop's morals: "It's wise to turn circumstances to good account."

JOHN S. MORGAN

Contents

AESOP'S FABLES
in
the
Executive
Suite

"It's easier to give advice than to take it."

Belling the Cat

Four mice told the fifth of their peers:
"Bell the cat and help stop our fears."
The fifth said, "That is nice.
I sure like your advice.
But not for me — get volunteers."

Aesop's Moral: "It's easier to give advice than to take it."

The Contemporary Illustration

Sometimes it's easier to write a book like this about promotion than actually to win a better job.

So, should you put this volume aside right now? Obviously, I hope not. But you should judge my advice for its practicality, long-term impact and psychological soundness. And, you should weigh carefully the advice from associates, using the same criteria. Problems arise with both giving and taking advice. But for now let's concentrate on aspects of taking counsel.

Ralph R. consulted with colleagues because he became the victim of a situation with political implications which he felt too inexperienced to handle on his own. He found himself involved in an organizational change that arbitrarily and unreasonably put him at a reporting level two steps below his former status, even though he continued to do the same work. (If this sounds preposterous, it is, but nevertheless it happens, especially in large companies.)

While Ralph's monthly salary wasn't cut, the lower reporting arrangements created several real difficulties. His pay became red-circled or a special case, meaning that he would probably have to wait longer for his next raise. His lower reporting level put him at a lower participation point in the pot for the year end bonus. He lost a good secretary because her grade was tied to his level. When his level fell, so did her grade. She too was red-circled on salary. But there was extensive movement among secretaries in the company, so she got a new job with a boss whose level matched her grade.

Ralph R. wondered if he should look for a job with a better reporting level, even though he liked the work he had been doing and would have preferred to continue doing it if the other factors had not changed. He hoped to stay in the company, so he made discreet inquiries among associates.

Their counsel boiled down to this: Sit tight; another reorganization is inevitable, and your job level may be restored. Ralph surprised himself to discover that he didn't like the advice. A "sea change" had occurred in his attitudes. At some point in stewing over his situation he had grown psychologically tuned to wanting a new job. He had several reasons for this new feeling: The reorganization had been unfair to him; he had been doing the same thing for seven years and needed a change; he was bored.

So he ignored his friends' counsel and went job hunting inside the company and elsewhere. He eventually found something outside that represented a modest promotion. Within a year, another reorganization did occur at his former company; his old job was restored to its former level. However, it was too late by then for Ralph, as the people whose advice he had scorned pointed out to him, none too subtly.

Did Ralph err in not following their advice? From a practical standpoint, probably yes. In moving, he gave up several advantages, such as seniority and eight years toward a pension — time which would have to be sacrificed. But from the standpoint of psychological soundness he was probably correct in moving. He had worked himself up emotionally to a state where he could no longer perform effectively on the old job. He was still young enough (thirty-four) to build satisfactory seniority and pension credits with his new employer, so the long-term impact of his decision was not disastrous.

Most situations are not clear-cut when advice is needed; that's why you seek counsel. In the long run, however, the person principally involved must make the decision — and no one else. Ralph's colleagues couldn't know or appraise his feelings about the job. While emotions should remain muted as much as possible in career situations, they nevertheless play a big part in the ultimate judgment, as in Ralph's case.

So, weigh advice in terms of your balanced best interests.

Yet it's wise to accept advice when you can because there's no better way to make friends than to ask it and no better way to keep friends than to follow it. Bernard Haldane, a New York-based executive recruiter or "career developer" as he prefers to call it, points out a sometimes overlooked benefit of counsel-taking: "If you take the man's advice he becomes obligated to help you fulfill the results which the advice should have made easier to attain."

Ed J. learned the wisdom of this. He heard of an opening as a vice president's statistical analyst. He didn't know the man personally and cast about for a mutual acquaintance. He found one and asked him how to go about presenting his case to the vice president.

"I can do better than give you advice," the acquaintance replied. "I'll present your case for you." He did and Ed got the promotion.

In asking for and following advice, consider the disinterestedness of the source. A factor in Ralph's decision to ignore his colleagues lay in the suspicion that they wanted him to do nothing because they would welcome his sitting out the competitive job sweepstakes. The reorganization had so unsettled the whole structure that no job was completely safe. Ed had a few qualms, too, when the acquaintance went far beyond normal custom in presenting his case for him. But everything worked out well. Some people are nice.

Advice may be poor for psychological reasons. Young Tom Y. was outraged when his older friend Walt R. didn't get the sales managership. Although Tom had held his job for only about a year, he had been with the firm long enough to believe that Walt was the better choice for the promotion than the man who actually won it. Tom commiserated with Walt. They discussed the subject frequently at their lunches which they had fallen into the habit of having together. Their families began socializing, although Walt was ten years Tom's senior.

When things went poorly for Tom under the new regime, it became Walt's turn to commiserate.

"By God," he would say, "you're getting a raw deal. If I were running this show, things would be different."

Tom proposed that they both complain to top management.

"That would look like sour grapes coming from me," said Walt, "because I had reason to think I would become sales manager. But you aren't in the same spot. You would be more disinterested. They might listen to you."

Spurred by his genuine friendship and admiration for Walt, plus more than a touch of self-interest, Tom did lodge a complaint with top management. Nothing apparently resulted from it—until a few months later when the sales manager, still in his job, suggested that Tom "might find better opportunities elsewhere."

Although some may attempt to do so, not many of us mice want to—or should—bell the cat.

Modern Precept for Promotion: "Judge advice from associates for its practicality, impact and soundness."

"Don't guess at the whole from the parts."

The Blind Men and the Elephant

One blind man felt Elephant's trunk.
Another touched his body's hunk
They guessed from head to leg:
A tree, a rock, a keg.
'Til Elephant trumpeted "Bunk!"

Aesop's Moral: "Don't guess at the whole from the parts."

The Contemporary Illustration

George E. didn't like his manufacturing job with an appliance manufacturer. He wished to return to his real love, engineering, but he didn't want to leave the company and he didn't want to foul the relationship with his boss by telling him that he preferred something else.

George passed the word of his dissatisfaction to a couple of friends in the organization who he knew were discreet and hoped for something to happen. Nothing did. When he learned that somebody else had won a promotion to a newly created position in engineering, he was sick. The job was just what he had been looking for. He visited the engineering manager and told him of his disappointment.

"I feel as badly as you do, George," said the manager. "I had no idea you were looking. I would have considered you seriously if I had known."

George's emissaries had been too discreet. Actually, they had done almost nothing to help him. When George had emphasized discretion, they had taken that as an excuse for inaction. Job searching is rarely easy. Nobody likes to do it without powerful motivation — for example, because you need a new spot for yourself.

If you want a better job, the first thing you must do is to let the strategic people know you're looking. This is particularly important if you seek to remain with your present employer. When you don't do this, you grope in the dark like the blind men.

George had never before tried moving within the same organization and missed a critical opportunity. As soon as he had decided that he wanted to change, he should have made that desire widely known — and to his boss first of all.

In large organizations especially, no job-hopping onus is attached to a man or woman who moves fairly often, provided he remains in the family. Sidney K. was an ambitious young man who made a point to tell every new boss early in their association that he sought promotions, preferably in the new man's component, but elsewhere if that failed. Did anyone ever seem to resent so direct an approach?

"Never that I could see," answers Sid. "A few showed surprise, but I think they were far more impressed than annoyed."

He never let a chance slip by to let the boss and other suitable people know he wanted to move upward. He climbed to steadily improving jobs four times in six years as a result.

"I use the old-boy network," Sid confides. "As I get more exposure, more people, particularly my present manager and former bosses, know what I can do. When an opening comes up, they will think of me. I do this 'selling' with managers only — people in a position to hire others. It's largely a waste of time to have non-managers 'looking' for you. I never had one help me to land another job. You have to deal directly with the guy who has the jobs."

Sid refuses to touch his company's formal job searching organization. "You might as well go to an outside executive recruiter," he comments. "Furthermore, this makes you go searching with hat in hand. If you use the old-boy route, the job is more apt to come looking for you. Furthermore, people with jobs to fill like to put people they know in them. Many managers go to our formal recruiting setup only as a last resort because that outfit is almost certain to dig up people they never heard of."

Sid adds another point in favor of his old-boy method. "A friend is more likely to level with you about the position he's offering simply because he's a friend, or at least an acquaintance. You get more reliable information using my methods."

George still demurred at letting his own boss know he was unhappy. "Forget it," counters Sid. "He'll probably find out about it eventually anyhow, but then he'll really be mad because he learned you were going behind his back. Tell him. He probably wants to move, too."

Certainly, more people do move these days. A recent survey of 1,000 business executives revealed that one-third of them occupied jobs that hadn't existed before. A Labor Department study showed that 71 million people in the United States labor force held jobs for 4.2 years on the average, vs. 4.6 years on the average only 3 years earlier.

Another Labor Department survey showed a man in his early twenties could expect to change jobs six or seven times during his lifetime. Instead of thinking of a career, people are beginning to think of serial careers. And you need far more and far better information under those circumstances.

In the fable of the "Wolf in Sheep's Clothing," I will discuss the problem of deceptive information. "The Blind Men and the Elephant" fable points up a broader difficulty — simply the acquisition of enough reliable facts.

George didn't have enough because he had tackled the challenge too diffidently, too obliquely. When you seek a better job, either with your present employer or another, you need to mount a vigorous and frontal attack, first to know what's available and second to assure that your availability is known.

The old-boy network performs double duty if you seek a job within the same company. It alerts you to what's opening, and it automatically makes the right people aware that you want a new opportunity. You can use it, for the same roles, but on a more limited scale, in searches in other companies. Unless you're very unusual, your old-boy network isn't likely to be as extensive outside as inside. In looking outside, your problem lies largely in finding suitable openings. Nobody has found a sure-fire method of doing this.

Aside from friends, the best source appears to be help-wanted ads in publications serving your line of work, in metropolitan newspapers, and in the *Wall Street Journal*. Professional recruiting firms are in the business of offering this service, but they receive mixed reviews from the people that have used them to hunt for jobs.

George registered with one after the engineering job fiasco, but it gave him little help. It sent him on two fruitless interviews and then appeared to lose interest in him. On the other hand, the same agency approached Sid with a proposal for a job with a competing company. When Sid investigated and turned down the proposition, he commented, "Head hunters are best for a company trying to fill a job, not for a guy looking for one. Recruiters' fees come largely from the employer, not from the individual, so their emphasis is not surprising. If an individual who registers with them happens to have qualifications which match an opening that one of their clients has, everybody's happy — and lucky. Unfortunately, such a match-up doesn't happen too often."

George finally got a lead on a job by answering a blind ad in the *Wall Street Journal*. When he learned the identity of the potential employer as a rival appliance maker after it had contacted him, he remembered a college friend, Irving H., who worked there. At last, he got smart and used the old-boy technique effectively.

Although the position was not in Irving's component, he

was able to scout around and assemble information in four areas vital to George:

- The job's future attractions.
- Conversely, the potential pitfalls in the job.
- The political crosscurrents that could affect the job.
- George's chances of getting the position, if he wanted it.

The first three informational categories, with either the same employer or a potential new one, will help determine whether even to pursue the opportunity. The fourth category proves important, as we shall see, in fine-tuning the applicant's degree of aggressiveness in seeking the job.

If the new job is with the same employer, you can probably assess your friend's efficiency and accuracy in information gathering in the light of your own knowledge. If another employer is involved, you must rely heavily on faith.

But even with good and accurate information, you must interpret it correctly. Oddly, the employer himself may distort your judgment, especially if he urgently needs to fill the position and oversells it. You may err in allowing a new position's substantially increased salary to over-influence you.

Irving reported to George that the position involved design, installation and debugging of new equipment. To George, its attractions lay in the creativity required, the variety of the assignments and the fact that he would be on his own to a large extent.

These characteristics also held dangers for the incumbent. The employer couldn't afford many errors. Three people who had held the job in the past five years had left. This rightly disturbed George until he learned that the three had been younger men frustrated by the seeming dead end of the position. Before the last three, an engineer had filled it admirably for twenty years before his retirement.

That the position tended to be a dead end, not leading to higher jobs in the company, did not worry George unduly. At forty-five he knew he did not want to become a manager, which would normally be the next rung in the ladder. He sought an interesting position in engineering as an individual contributor.

Irving's appraisal of the political crosscurrents on the proposed new job seemed reassuring. The person holding the position would report to the vice president for engineering, a thirty-six-year-old member of the family which founded and still owned the controlling interest in the appliance manufacturer. George liked the young scion when he met him and learned he held impeccable engineering credentials as an MIT graduate. George scarcely considered the fact that the man belonged to a faction of his family that was trying to oust rival members in a internecine conflict that had smoldered for several years. Because Irving estimated that the engineering vice president's side would win, George dismissed the matter.

The time comes in every hunt for a better job when the applicant must decide whether he wants a particular opportunity or not, even before it is actually offered to him. If he doesn't want it, he should drop it. If he is hesitant, he should probably also drop it because half measures will rarely win a promotion. If he decides he wants it, he must appraise one more aspect of the situation.

This is an analysis of his chances of being offered the job. If the odds are bad, the applicant should probably forget the whole thing, not wasting his time and energies. But if the odds are fair to good, he should go all-out to win. Irving estimated the odds as good that George would be offered the job.

Because of the engineering fiasco with his own company, George determined not to make the mistake of half measures again. He went all-out, enlisting Irving's support. George got the job, but he also got trouble. The internecine warfare that he had dismissed as irrelevant for him turned out to be the central fact in his new position. Within a year, the engineering vice president's group had lost out in the intramural squabble. All the important nonfamily employees with connections with the losing faction found themselves either out of work or stymied in their career.

George's fate became the latter. He lost his equipment development job and returned to a humdrum post in manufacturing, not much different from the one he had left in the first company.

George had overlooked the key aspect of the new position, just as the blind men had in examining the elephant.

Modern Precept for Promotion: "Know and appraise as many of the facts and circumstances as possible about the better job you seek."

"Handsome is as handsome does."

Brother and Sister

> Of the twins, the daughter was quite plain,
> While the son was handsome but too vain.
> "Let him boast of his looks,"
> Said Dad. "You mind your books
> For true beauty is bred in the brain."

Aesop's Moral: "Handsome is as handsome does."

The Contemporary Illustration

As a junior in college, Perry B. led a campaign that resulted in an unpopular dean's resignation.

He never realized the real reasons for his success in the matter of the dean. As a clean-cut youth with good but not outstanding grades, he had quietly asked for an interview with the college president and had presented him with a petition signed by 500 students listing the grievances against the man. Perry didn't know that the president already held many of the same objections to him and planned to drop him quietly at the beginning of the next school year. After successfully resisting so many unreasonable demands from students, the wise official gladly agreed to one that he knew had merit. He also shrewdly sponsored a student as leader who would be a welcome relief to the radicals he had had to deal with. Without Perry's realization, the president cannily made some moves that assured Perry the class presidency in his senior year.

With such collegiate credentials, Perry easily found a job upon graduation — with a stock brokerage firm. His self-assurance impressed the assistant sales manager, and Perry soon became the assistant when the latter moved up to sales manager.

Yet after two years without another promotion, Perry decided that the manager was blocking his progress. He quit to become the San Francisco manager of bond sales for another firm, at the age of twenty-five. In his former job, the sales manager had directed nearly all of the bond sales activity, but Perry so effectively conveyed the impression to his new employer that he had concentrated on bonds that he convinced even himself.

In San Francisco three thousand miles from the New York home office, Perry got by for a while. A less vain man might have panicked, but Perry never did as he struggled to learn the intricacies of the bond market. While he was learning, he made several expensive errors. The first brought a worried phone call from New York; the second a critical call from the managing partner, which Perry felt he handled very well.

"I calmed the old boy down," he confided to his secretary. "The mistake was a back-room slipup on the New York end, not here."

But the third error brought the managing partner to San Francisco in person. Perry was astounded to find himself fired. Perry had talked and charmed his way to a good impression, but he had not performed to make a good one.

Many vain people can last longer than Perry because they shrewdly do only those things that they know they perform well. Oliver H. learned this ploy almost to perfection.

As a reporter on a business magazine, Oliver wrote unexceptional articles, but they pleased the advertisers and the advertising sales staff. With the passing years, he wrote less and less and became a kind of contact man and adjunct of the sales staff. He would get a list of potential or troublesome advertisers, call, write or visit them, looking for a story. Of course, all the stories he dug up complimented the advertisers; praising their product, lauding their management skills or finding something good to say about them if neither their products were outstanding nor their management methods noteworthy.

He would then bundle up his notes, product brochures, management speeches and anything else he could find and give them to the newest man on the staff.

"Here, son, I've got to be out of town next week; see what you can make of all this. I think there's a good story in Acme's new line of fasteners."

Nine times out of ten the young neophyte would struggle to work up something. Oliver would thank him profusely, show the story to sales and then turn it in virtually unchanged to the editor. Four times out of five, the editor would protest.

"I can't use this crap about Acme," he would wail. "There's not a thing new here."

Oliver would make soothing noises. "I know, I know, but they gave me a call on this (a lie — Oliver had called them), what could I do?"

"You could tell them to take a flying leap."

"You know I couldn't do that. The ad boys kind of like it."

"Yeah, I'll bet they do. You showed this to them didn't you?"

"Of course, I'm the liaison with the business side." Oliver smiled because he was baiting the editor over a sore point. He had wrangled himself the liaison arrangement to the intense displeasure of the editor.

But the editor knew he had lost that one and didn't rise to the lure. "Who wrote this for you?"

"That new fellow on the staff, young what's-his-name."

"I make the assignments around here. The next puff piece you dig up, write yourself. That's an assignment."

"Yassuh, boss, massah." Oliver bowed with mock obsequiousness and backed out of the editor's office. Oliver had heard that before, too. His other response to it was, "I'm too busy and National hoped this could make the next issue. I've got to be out of town for the next three days."

There was no way to shame Oliver. His conceit was impervious to insult. He had found his niche as a shill for the advertising department, and that's all he would do. He became so good at it that when the editorship became vacant his sales allies won the coveted post for him.

But here Oliver ran into trouble for a while. The editor was supposed to write editorials. Oliver's proved so poor that even his sales allies grew uneasy. Eventually, a managing editor had to be named who could perform the editor's usual duties. Being a figurehead bothered Oliver not at all. He continued his work as shill, delighted to retain the title of editor.

Yet, what if Oliver had taken the trouble to learn to write at least passably well! What a trade magazine editor he could have been. As it was, he remained a hack. Not surprisingly, his magazine eventually died, from lack of nutrition at the top.

While many successful people have their full share of conceit, most also have enough intelligence to recognize that good performance must enter the picture somewhere to generate promotions. In small doses, vanity does no harm and may even spur people to develop skills that had been weak so that their peers might have more cause to admire them.

The ideal person, perhaps, has no conceit. Stephen Vincent Benét, in his poem "*John Brown's Body*," believed that Ulysses S. Grant was such an individual:

> There is no brilliant lamp in that dogged mind
> And no conceit of brilliance to shake the hand,
> But hand and mind can use the tools they get.
> . . . The quiet, equable, deadly holder-on.

Those attributes promoted him to the U.S. presidency.

Modern Precept for Promotion: "You may look like a success but the real payoff lies in how you perform."

"Strength is in unity."

The Bundle of Sticks

To quarrelsome sons who fell out,
Their father had these words to shout:
"A single stick soon snaps.
A bundle takes all raps.
Unity — that's what strength's about."

Aesop's Moral: "Strength is in unity."

The Contemporary Illustration

The dictionary defines unity as "oneness resulting from harmony."

Who denies that such a state is desirable and leads to strength? The problem lies not in accepting this concept's truth but in achieving it, especially to further your own advancement. A common way to unite with others is to have a common purpose. But, if your goal is promotion, that usually narrows the possibilities that your advancement will serve others' ambitions as well.

Yet Tina N. found a way to harness other people's self-interest with her own to win promotions for all. She was a registered representative (as stock brokers are formally called in the trade) with a West Coast-based brokerage house. Because probably less than 10 per cent of all such reps are women, she felt unhappy as a member of a minority in the field.

"In my city, there wasn't a single woman who was an officer in her firm," she says. "I resigned from one larger house when men stole two of my big institutional accounts. The name of the game at that firm was not ethics. While the firm I joined next (and which still employs her) was much better, I still felt unhappy."

She formed Women Registered Representatives, Inc. and offered membership to any woman in her city who had spent five years or more dealing with investors on a commission basis. The group then began to campaign for a better deal for their sex.

"We brought unethical practices to the attention of the firms involved," Tina recalls. "We got a couple of stories in the newspapers about our organization and its purposes. We pointed out that the giant

Merrill Lynch Pierce, Fenner & Smith, Inc. employed only about 150 women among its 5,000 representatives. We named many other firms that had no women reps. We publicized the facts about the lack of women as officers in brokerage firms."

When Tina was invited to speak on the subject before a meeting of the security analysts in her city, she felt she had at last arrived. Indeed she had. Eventually, she became a vice president of her firm, and four other members of her organization shortly became officers in their houses. From a membership of only nine when she started the group, it grew to twenty in just three years. "I learned first hand that there is strength in unity," says Tina.

You don't have to organize a formal association to achieve unity. You can do it through mutual aid, between two people, as we will learn in the "Dog in the Manger" and other fables. A word of warning, however: Mutual aid must bring mutual benefit to prove successful. That was lacking in the tandem arrangement between Walt R. and Tom Y. in "Belling the Cat". The benefits went just one way, to Walt. Tom was too inexperienced to realize Walt had victimized him.

Even when the benefits seem to go in only one direction, we'll learn that both parties gain in the successful cases; even when the benefit isn't superficially apparent.

Still another route opens for you to use unity as a way to promotion. This lies in achieving unity among your employees to prove that you are promotable. After her success with the association of women representatives, Tina's firm put her in charge of selling new issues, with an all-male sales force.

"The job was something of a put-down," she recalls because there weren't many new issues coming out. "I suspected but couldn't prove that this was some sort of punishment for my 'Women's Lib' activities. Also, I had several of the firm's misfits on my team. At first I was mad as the devil, but then I realized I would prove nothing positive by bitching about the assignment. I had nothing to lose by trying to make something of it because my predecessor had flopped, and I could do scarcely worse than he."

One of the members on that team, who succeeded her to the job after she became vice president, recalls those days.

"She was a dream to work for, or rather with. Sort of like Joan of Arc, with humor. 'Well, fellows,' she said when she got us together for the first time, 'we're all in the doghouse, apparently, for one thing or another with a dog of an assignment like this. Let's make this the best doghouse in town for the best-of-breed winner of the show.' We did, too. Damn, but we had fun!"

Books have been (and will be) written on how to be a good manager.

Underlying all the advice, however, is one basic precept — which will make you a better manager and further your career — learn to persuade others to do willingly what you want them to do. In other words, get unity. You can accomplish this by mastering nine basic principles of persuasion.

The first is to state your conclusion — make crystal clear where you stand and why you take that position. Do not let the facts alone speak for themselves. Your listeners may not draw the same conclusions you do from the facts. They may not have all the background you have on the situation and are not equipped to draw a fully accurate conclusion. But your conclusions must have logic and must respond to a need.

Tina persuaded other women to join with her because she had logic on her side and she responded to a need that they all felt.

The second principle of persuasion stems from the first. Emotions persuade more effectively than facts, particularly in the short run. Of course, you must have facts, but you need an emotional catalyst to leaven them. Facts come across best when you can impart an ideal quality to them.

Tina did this by tieing in her campaign with the broader one of equality for women. She avoided some of the extreme manifestations of the movement. "We're not burning our bras," she promised.

The third principle of persuasion is to take your time. Even intelligent people have trouble with new ideas. If you hope to get new or complicated concepts across to others quickly, you're doomed to disappointment.

Tina had the greatest trouble with this one. She was impatient and tended to show it. Fortunately, some of the other members of her group showed her the folly of impatience and persuaded her to curb herself more.

The next principle involves repetition and anticipation. You have to repeat your message in as many different ways as possible.

Tina proved a master at this. She gave her theme many different twists and emphases. She used many different forums to tell her views.

Expect resistance — the fifth principle of persuasion. Tina did, of course. The person who leads and never encounters resistance is either fooling himself or operating in an authoritarian situation where the resistance is hidden and waiting to surface.

Strive for positive personal involvement. For this sixth principle, Tina sought a male investment representative as an ally. She initially won over the president of her own firm. When he came on board, he helped her recruit the head of another. Eventually she enlisted five male presidents of brokerage firms to help actively in her campaign.

She learned another thing, too. Each new male recruit proved easier to enlist than the previous one. So, the sixth principle of persuasion closely relates to the old bandwagon rule of politics — get a few and you'll soon have a flock; get a flock and you'll soon draw a crowd.

Show that the desired action is possible. The seventh persuasion principle follows logically. When you meet the inevitable resistance, overcome it with personal involvement. True personal involvement will prove impossible unless you can show the feasibility of what you want done.

Tina showed that some investors preferred women to men. When she became a vice president, she demonstrated managerial abilities. And the other women in her city who became officers performed well, too.

State your motives frankly. We often lose sight of this eighth principle. Many of us must think our motives of self-interest are dishonorable. Why? Self-interest motivates almost everything we do. If kept within bounds, self-interest is normal.

Tina never erred in claiming she had no self-interest. On the contrary, she almost flouted it from the start. That proved a persuasive tactic because the men whose prejudices she sought to overcome understood her motives. They knew they would share them if they were women. Therefore, they tended to feel sympathy toward her, in spite of themselves.

Guard your credibility. This ninth major persuasion principle is the most important of all. If Tina hadn't stated her motives frankly, she would have unwittingly undermined her credibility.

Without it, all the managerial skills in the world won't achieve the unity needed to advance your career.

Modern Precept for Promotion: "Gain converts in your campaign for promotion."

"Familiarity serves to overcome dread."

The Camel

Man at first feared the Camel, you see,
Because it looked as fierce as could be.
Fright eased, to say the least,
When he learned that the beast
Was a horse designed by committee.

Aesop's Moral: "Familiarity serves to overcome dread."

The Contemporary Illustration

Over cocktails that night, Quincy didn't mention until the second martini the subject that had agitated him all day.

"They offered me the managership of the Massachusetts plant today." He tried to sound casual.

"Darling, how wonderful! When do you start?" Marie leaned forward, smiling and expectant.

"Wait a minute! I haven't accepted yet. Told them I wanted to think it over."

"Of course." Marie nodded after a moment. "You don't want to seem too eager."

"Well, I'm not too eager. The kids for one thing. We'd have to change schools, right in the middle of the school year, too. And little Marie has had a tough enough time getting started in the first grade. What would it do to her to have to change so soon? And Jack has such a tough time adjusting to anything new."

Marie held up a finger for silence and went to the family room door to close it.

"Marie's completely engrossed in television, but you never can tell. Jack is at his Boy Scout meeting," she said. "All I can comment is, that it might do them good to change schools. I think the teaching competence in this system is below average. That's led to Marie's problems, not any psychological thing, particularly."

"There's something else that bothers me, really." Quincy stared into his martini glass as though he'd find the answer there. "It's money. The base salary would be only one thousand a year higher than I'm getting now."

"But you'd get much more in a bonus," Marie said triumphantly.

"Not necessarily. That's the rub. The Massachusetts plant is in trouble. It did poorly last year. There was no big bonus for anyone there."

Marie waved her glass. "It's obvious, then, why they want you — to turn the place around."

"Yes, but what if I don't turn it around? In fact, what if I flop?"

His wife rose and crossed to the sofa where he was seated. "Honey, this isn't like you. How many times have I heard you say — right in this room — what you'd do if you had a plant to manage of your own?" She put her arm across his shoulder. "This is your big chance, Quincy, the one you've been telling me you wanted."

"But I'm doing great here as the No. 2 man. Sure, I think Hansen's haywire on some things. But he's one of the top plant managers in the company, and we have one of the key plants. Massachusetts is the smallest shop in the whole chain. I hate to leave this place. Hansen can still teach me a lot, and we've only been here two years. I could even succeed him eventually."

Marie settled back on the couch. "You'll never succeed him unless you've managed a smaller plant well and on your own. They're grooming you for bigger things, darling, and this Massachusetts job is part of the grooming. That's obvious, isn't it?"

Of course it was obvious, even to Quincy J. Nevertheless, the offer of promotion had aroused a feeling of panic in him. He had not expected the chance for at least another year because tenure of at least three years in most positions was company policy. And in his wildest nightmare he hadn't dreamed of Massachusetts, a notoriously troubled plant.

"I wonder if Hansen wants to sidetrack me, even kill me in the company?" he muttered.

"Why?" Marie was genuinely puzzled. "He likes you, specifically asked for you as his assistant. He's told me he has had his eye on you ever since you worked for him on the training program. Quincy, he thinks you can turn the Massachusetts plant around, which apparently badly needs doing. He has confidence in you even if you don't have enough in yourself."

What really troubled Quincy? Like many sensitive and intelligent people, he feared change because it meant a shift to something unfamiliar. Let's examine what goes on psychologically when most of us face change, especially an unexpected change.

The human mind isn't tangible. It's a function not an entity. It's analogous to the speed of a car. The mind is the function of learning. It combines reason, reflection, intelligence, intellect, wile, perceptual and conceptual thinking, association of ideas, foresight, curiosity, purposefulness, self-control, conscience, sense of humor, creativity and appreciation.

The physical evolution of man has stood at an approximate standstill for 500,000 years, but not his mind's evolution. We have a written story of man — history — for only 7,000 years, 1 per cent of the human story. That 1 per cent indicates the extent of the evolution of the mind. In other words, most of the mind's evolution has taken place in only 1 per cent of man's time on earth.

Prehistoric man was probably an extreme communist — all for one, one for all. No marriage existed, but extreme promiscuity. The group mind prevailed, with little or no self-consciousness. His distinction from lower animals, while early, was blurred. The mind of the individual and the mind of the tribe were virtually indivisible.

The first nonconformists were individualists (whom we now accept as commonplace and admirable) and they gave in to self-interest (which we now accept as the criterion by which most men form their judgments).

The first nonconformists were either expelled or became kings, chiefs or witch doctors. It's no accident that no records exist for tribes who expelled their nonconformists. Those who became leaders changed their tribes, which usually led to greater things. Those without a nonconforming leader faded into oblivion.

As one or a few minds made new discoveries and initiated changes, other quick minds accepted the changes, and eventually most minds climbed to a new plateau.

And of course the converse can occur. With no or little change, a race, a nation, a company or a person will atrophy. Australian aborigines, Manadarin China, many companies and countless individuals have suffered this psychological fate. A deliberate attempt to slow psychological growth may also lead to atrophy — or revolt.

From these observations and from Quincy's dilemma, we can extrapolate the following conclusions about the individual's psychological reaction to change:

1. The prospect for change upsets most people until they know it doesn't threaten their status or well-being. This disturbed Quincy more than any other single factor. He enjoyed good pay, high status and considerable prestige in his present job. Why jeopardize them with the ominous problems in Massachusetts?

2. Positive change stimulates most people. The present job had enormously stimulated Quincy, especially when he had first come on it two years earlier.

3. A lack of change dulls most people. In his previous assignment, Quincy had grown restive during the third year and had welcomed the promotion to assistant plant manager, to serve under a man he already knew and liked.

4. Change tends to have a "Pied Piper" effect; other changes follow good changes, and other people adopt those changes that prove promising. With Hansen's encouragement, Quincy had inaugurated a new inventory control system that had been adopted in all the company's plants. Quincy still privately marvelled that he had conceived it and implemented it. Significantly, the development had occurred within a year of his becoming assistant plant manager.

5. It's more comfortable to prepare for and accept change than to wait until it is forced upon us. This was another factor that disturbed Quincy about Massachusetts, almost as much as the threat to his status. He had not expected the offer. During cocktails with his wife, he was still trying to accustom himself to the idea.

6. Man has the wit to cope with change. In contrast animals must await, unconsciously, their adaptation to their changing environment across evolution's course spread over numberless generations. Quincy knew that he had solved known problems in the past. The trouble was that he did not know exactly what Massachusetts's problems were, except that they were severe and had apparently defeated the present management there. Quincy didn't know if he had the experience or intelligence to succeed where others had failed — another reason for his self-doubt. He also read much management literature and had recently noted a study which found that one in three men promoted to plant manager or its equivalent — and believed to have the talent to handle the job — soon lost his appetite for the greater responsibility.

7. Change usually involves challenges to customs and habits which, while intangible, are tenacious. Although the company had long since expanded south and west and had moved its headquarters to New York City, it had originated in the Massachusetts location. As the "founding father," the plant enjoyed special status and retained management styles anachronistic in the rest of the company. Quincy suspected that this was part, or perhaps even most, of the problem. He dreaded tackling a situation like that, so new to his experience.

That night after dinner, Marie showed Quincy something Jack had obtained from his Boy Scout leader — four rules for survival if you get lost in the wilderness. They soon intrigued his father:

1. Stay calm. Panic accounts for 90 per cent of the problem.
2. Stay in one place. Don't go off in all directions. You will get no-where.

3. Keep dry and warm.
4. Have the will to live.

Marie didn't need to say it for he saw that these four rules can also be applied to survival in facing the unknown:

1. Stay calm. Panic won't help. The change may benefit you.
2. Appraise the situation with hard thought. Get facts about the unknown. When you know more about it, what will you, tentatively, do about it?
3. Some principles and convictions — honesty, compassion, etc. — never change. Hang on to them no matter what else is changing.
4. Have the will to survive. Flight from the unknown or listless resignation to it will not help you prosper with change. Seek to control it, not to let it control you.

The next day, Quincy said he would accept the new job on two conditions: that he was given time to investigate the problems in the Massachusetts plant and that he had carte blanche to deal with them as he saw fit. His conditions were accepted.

Modern Precept for Promotion: "Quickly make the unknown known to master the new job."

"Don't take all the credit for yourself."

The Cock, the Ass and the Lion

The Cock crowed long; the Ass brayed 'til hoarse.
The Lion ran as though from the force.
"Scared him!" cried Cock and Ass.
They did not know, alas,
That the Lion was just bored, of course.

Aesop's Moral: "Don't take all the credit for yourself."

The Contemporary Illustration

Kevin O. was the only person in the audience who neither laughed nor smiled when his boss on the podium ended a graceful speech accepting the company's man-of-the-year award by saying he was "tops in humility."

Kevin believed that his boss had stolen the award from him. The man had claimed credit for more than a score of cost-saving ideas that had originated with Kevin. But what could a mere employee do?

For the time being he just smoldered, not wanting to air the issue in public. For a while, he considered quitting, but he finally decided on a different approach. In private later, he confronted his boss:

"I was disappointed that you didn't give me a little of the credit in your man-of-the-year acceptance."

The manager held out his hands palm upward. "Kev, I did. I said the whole thing was a group effort."

"If I'm a group, that's right. But I consider myself a person. I didn't hear my name mentioned once."

"Kev, I can see you're upset, and I'm sorry. But I couldn't name just you up there. Then, the rest of the gang would be upset."

"I don't see why." Kevin hunched forward in his chair. "They had nothing to do with any of those ideas that won you the award."

Now, the boss edged forward. "Wait a minute! You were just accusing me of credit hogging. This whole thing was a group deal. Sure, you had the lead role in it, but it was a team effort."

And so it went. Each parted with the issue unresolved and with each sincerely believing that the other had maligned him. Over almost any period of time, many sharp edges of truth subtly change, in the view of the beholder. The facts in this case were that Kev had assumed the lead role, as his manager acknowledged, but all of the other people in the group had also made contributions, although none of them major. If the manager had cited anyone in his acceptance talk, he should have mentioned Kev. On the other hand, the manager thought — however mistakenly — that he had bypassed trouble by not naming anyone.

Although the kind of credit problem Kev and his manager had embroiled themselves in turns up most typically, you should guard against other variations, too.

Outright theft of accounts, star employees and the like, surface more frequently than anyone cares to admit. Denigration is another scourge that I'll deal with in the fable of the "Snake and the File." For the moment, I'll just say that in the denigration game nobody can make real gains, just illusory victories that seem like wins in comparison with the loser's lowered status. But the "victor" has lost a little too in his perception of himself and probably in how others now see him.

I call a special type of theft "hoarded credit," and I'll deal with it more fully in the fable of the "Wind and the Sun." Favoritism typically causes this phenomenon whereby the giver of favors now implies that the receiver must return one later on demand. In theory this sounds reasonable, but in practice the hoarded credit often evaporates. A variation of hoarded credit that's just as ephemeral involves the building up of unnecessary expenses that can be "reduced" painlessly when the inevitable call comes for belt-tightening. I'll discuss that one in the fable of the "Dog in the Manger."

All these dubious practices aim at job advancement or similar personal gain. Aside from questions of ethics and morality, you should avoid them because they seldom work for long. Of the lessons that Kevin's case teaches, four stand out:

1. Be generous on the side of indulgence in giving credit to others. Although Kevin's manager erred in this regard, Kev had brought some of the trouble upon himself. He had always been a loner, never cooperating well on group projects, always jealous of his supposed rights. The manager didn't mention his name out of spite and — more importantly — out of stupidity. It would have cost him nothing at least to have mentioned Kevin's name. The boss would have gained a loyal and gifted ally if he had suggested Kev as the man-of-the-year winner in his stead. A manager, particularly, reaps real rewards in having gifted people work for him because they ease his job and contribute to his success.

Spite and stupidity, leavened with vanity, proved so potent a brew that it impelled Kev, introverted and normally inarticulate, to take his case to the company president. While that worthy's discreet investigation didn't support Kevin completely, it did reveal that Kev had imaginative cost-cutting talents which the company didn't fully employ. Kev soon won a lateral transfer to a component where the president thought his abilities would find better use. His former manager didn't lose his job or his man-of-the-year award, but he never won another plaque, nor did he ever get promoted again.

2. Never steal credit yourself — if only to avoid retaliation. In taking undue credit you purloin part of another reputation, more valuable to most of us than material things. Retribution in some form is almost certain.

In this regard, consider the danger of looking ridiculous in trying to gain credit by jumping on the bandwagon. The classic case occurred in an early film version of *The Taming of the Shrew*. The credits read, "By William Shakespeare, with additional dialogue by Sam Taylor."

3. Know your colleagues — and boss. Let's face it, some people are unscrupulous. Know who might try to steal credit and take reasonable precautions.

While it pays to be vigilant, note that I say "reasonable precautions." Oddly, Kevin was overly vigilant, if anything. He constantly looked for burglars under the bed, to the extent that he never examined the ceiling — through which his boss entered. Of course, you can overdo vigilance in other ways.

You can spend so much time at it that you have little for anything else. Commonly, the overly vigilant person does poorly at teamwork and other cooperative efforts. That was Kev's problem, partially solved in his new department when he became an individual contributor, responsible for nothing but to come up with cost-saving ideas.

4. Take certain safeguards. You can relax your vigilance if you adopt a few common-sense precautions.

The first is to sign your work. You can do this easily if you must write reports, memos or letters about it. Sometimes it pays to prepare such a document to be certain you do stake your claim, even if it serves no other purpose.

A second kind of safeguard is to let significant people know what you're doing in general terms. Choose such confidants with care, to avoid giving the game away to a potential thief. Your aim here is to say politely, "Keep off the grass," and to build evidence of your activity in case of future need.

Many people naturally think first of secrecy as the ultimate precaution. Yet booby traps lie everywhere here. In a work environment it's difficult, if not impossible, to maintain secrecy. Just keeping something secret serves as a challenge for some people to try to unmask the mystery. Secrecy will also probably alienate you from many of your fellow employees. It's far more effective usually to speak freely about your project in general but to say as little as possible about it in particular.

But the ultimate safeguard is trust. If you're generous in giving credit to others, if you never usurp credit yourself, and if you are a genuine friend of your associates, most will return the favor.

Modern Precept for Promotion: "Give credit generously and it will be returned."

"Use your wits."

The Crow and the Pitcher

So how did the smart crow get a drink?
The pitcher's liquid was low. Now think!
No, he never spilled it!
With pebbles he filled it
Until water rose up to the brink.

Aesop's Moral: "Use your wits."

The Contemporary Illustration

Practically everyone is innovative, but to varying degrees. Yet, few people make full use of their innovative faculties, especially when it comes to winning a promotion. It's really irrelevant how much creativity you have in this area; the important thing is to use more fully what you do possess.

Many have the feeling that using your wits to get ahead amounts to trickery or even dishonesty. Only when you use your wits to devise dishonest or unethical schemes are you guilty. To gain advancement by such means represents a debasement of one of man's noblest gifts, creativity. So many legitimate uses exist for creativity. Why concentrate on the illegitimate?

Other people object to analyzing the innovative faculty for fear of damaging some mysterious, intuitive and subconscious process. If you share that uneasiness, think of creativity as a kind of sight. Like eyesight, creative vision often can be improved — primarily by analysis and exercise.

An overly narrow understanding of creativity leads to the reluctance to analyze it — and thus, often to improve it. It helps, then, to understand the characteristics of innovation, to know better how to use the faculty to advance yourself.

The creative person can employ any, some or even all of about a dozen characteristics:

Use the familiar for unfamiliar purposes. Trevor G. had a job selling in a bookstore. He noted the great popularity of books relating to household budgeting. On the side, he started a mail advisory service on household budgeting, with modest charges. The simple idea hit the bull's eye; it flourished from the start. He applied the trend he saw at the bookstore to an unfamiliar purpose, an information letter.

Hypothesize and suspend. When you hypothesize, you make assumptions from known truths. When you suspend, you stop and examine some of the hypotheses. Trev knew that many of the budgeting books were mediocre or even poor; yet they all sold well. The obvious hypothesis: People needed information on how to balance their budgets. When Trev then stopped to examine this obvious truth, he saw that the books weren't fully satisfying the need. Why? Because many were inadequate. Because a book soon got out of date like yesterday's newspaper as economic conditions changed. His solution: A good periodic advisory service to keep up with the times.

Get involved, then withdraw. Complete absorption alternates with withdrawal. This goes hand in hand with the preceding characteristic. Trev made full plans for his mail advisory service, then put them aside completely while he went on a two-week vacation. When he returned, he looked at them afresh, spotted some flaws and corrected them.

Use the phenomenon of autonomy. There comes a time when the solution separates itself from the creator. It begins to make suggestions, as it were, to its creator and takes part in developing itself. As with all good ideas, the advisory service soon took off. At first, Trev issued it quarterly. Demand grew so rapidly that he switched to an issue every two months, then monthly. General Motors' great inventor, Charles F. Kettering, referred to this phenomenon when he told associates, "Let the engine tell you what it needs."

Allow the idea to develop. This follows from the preceding characteristic. The creative person allows the solution to take part in developing itself; when it does, he knows he has a good idea. That's what Trev did with his advisory service.

Thus, creative people use thought processes that are not too unusual, even to you and me. They use the familiar. They hypothesize and examine the hypothesis. They get involved, but at times they stand back and let the situation take over. This last may seem spooky, but it's not. When you get a good idea, have you noticed how other ideas flow from it, almost spontaneously? This is an important asset for creative people.

Develop a sensitivity to problems. In other words, recognize when you have a problem. Trev was particularly attuned to the sale of household budgeting books because he had the problem personally. He had read everything on the subject that the store stocked, at first because he faced the challenge of balancing his own budget. Then it occurred to him to wonder why so many books appeared.

Learn to redefine problems. This is the ability to shift ideas and conceptions and in so doing to find a new or different way of solving a problem. He couldn't make ends meet on the job in the bookshop. In that field he knew he couldn't earn much more unless he owned the store himself, but he didn't have the capital to start his own.

But he did have enough capital to start the advisory service. He redefined the problem of balancing his budget by finding a new and added source of income. Within two years, he earned enough from the advisory service to quit his bookselling job and devote full time to what had been a sideline. Within ten years, he accumulated enough capital to open a specialized bookstore on how-to-do-it subjects which he hired someone else to manage for him.

Be flexible. Still another creative trait is willingness to consider a wide variety of approaches to a problem. Trevor showed flexibility because he was willing to look at his budget problem from a fresh viewpoint. In addition to that, he let the idea tell him what to do with it. And he later had the flexibility to open a specialized shop.

Be analytical. Skill in analyzing a situation is particularly important for the ambitious employee. Trev's analysis of why budgeting books came and went with such regularity led him to conclude that the time was ripe for a periodic service in this field.

Synthesize. This skill consists of pulling seemingly unrelated ideas into a new whole. From the book business, Trevor knew something about the mail advisory field. And he certainly knew about budgetary problems from his experience at home. He synthesized the two into his new endeavor.

Organize. Despite a popular impression to the contrary, an innovative person can rarely afford to be disorganized. Trevor, too, showed strong organizational ability, especially of his time. When he was following two careers while just starting in the mail order business, he had to balance his time like a juggler. He did it so successfully for two years that he could finally afford to drop the bookselling career.

Develop drive. This usually proves to be the most important quality of all to the innovatively ambitious person. More bright ideas have faded for lack of push than for any other reason. Trevor pushed, sometimes to the distress of his family and friends, but that's often the price that associates of energetic people have to pay. Their reward: The connection with a person on the move often serves as the catharsis in their own lives to get them moving, too.

Finally, while an analytical understanding of creativity is essential to develop your innovative abilities for advancement, you must use that understanding, too. A pianist who knows only the theories of piano playing won't play well unless he practices. Like the piano player, you must exercise your theories so that they become good practices, also.

Modern Precept for Promotion: "Innovation spurs advancement."

"No decision may be worse than the wrong decision."

The Dilemma of the Bat

The poor Bat could not make up his mind
To be bird or a beast, or what kind.
In caves he would wander
The better to ponder,
But he stayed there so long he grew blind.

Aesop's Moral: "No decision may be worse than the wrong decision."

The Contemporary Illustration

Dwight C. stopped in the men's room before going to the vice president's office. He washed his hands in an attempt to stop the sweating, and he applied a wet paper towel to his face. After a while his heartbeat slowed. He told himself sternly that he was fifty-two, an experienced businessman and the senior accountant in the department. Nevertheless he still felt like a boy at school summoned to the principal's office to be disciplined for some transgression.

Yet Dwight knew what the vice president wanted to see him about — "reorganization in accounting," he had said. Ever since the previous accounting manager had died unexpectedly three months earlier, his post had remained vacant. The vice president had taken over the job, "as acting manager, not the permanent head of the department," he had told him. Dwight's hopes for the position had waned as the weeks went by.

His wife had suggested that he ask for the post outright, but he didn't like doing that. Then she urged him to hunt for a job elsewhere. He had gone so far as to write a resume; he had not yet sent it to anybody. Now, perhaps the indecision that his wife decried would prove the patience he had always claimed his slowness to act really signified.

"Come in, come in," called the vice president, as Dwight stood uncertainly in his doorway. Dwight started toward the chair in front of the officer's desk.

"No, no, let's both sit on the couch," said the vice president, touching his arm. In the shift of direction, the accountant barked his shin against the edge of a coffee table in front of the couch. The pain was so sharp that he missed the other's first words.

". . . . appreciate your patience in waiting us out for a decision on this reorganization," he was saying.

Dwight's spirits lifted and the pain subsided. "I wanted to give you every chance to think this whole thing through," he said solemnly.

"Thank you." The vice president paused as he gazed out the window. "Have you ever run across a fellow named Charles Heller?"

Dwight frowned in anxious concentration. "No, I don't believe I have."

The other nodded as though he expected the answer. "He's a member of the accounting fraternity, too. He has been with Consolidated."

"Has been?"

"Yes. But he will be with us now — as of the first of the month. He'll join you and the others in accounting."

Dwight paused. The other said nothing, so he asked, "In what capacity?"

"He'll be manager of accounting, and you'll be promoted to manager of accounting programs. Congratulations." The vice president held out his hand, and the accountant shook it as he managed a smile.

"Will I be reporting to you, sir?" he asked in the fleeting hope that the answer might be yes.

"No, no — to Heller. And you'll like him. Very competent. Very decisive."

"Well, of course I'm disappointed," said Dwight.

The vice president examined something through the window. "But you never said you wanted the job."

"Well, no. I was on the verge of asking several times, but it didn't seem, uh, appropriate to." Then as often happens with diffident and normally inarticulate people, Dwight suddenly began to talk too much. All his frustrations and bitterness poured out.

When he had finally run down, the vice president said, "I'm glad we've had this chat, man. It gets things out in the light. But from all you've said and from what I've learned about you in our last three months of closer association, I think this new job will be right up your alley."

Dwight felt drained now, so only a trace of bitterness crept into his question, "What will this accounting programs job involve?"

The vice president assumed a judicious look as he lit a cigaret. Then he offered one to the other, grimacing his chagrin at the breach of etiquette, but Dwight shook his head, wondering why the man never remembered that he didn't smoke.

"We have some ideas on this," said the official, "but I'd like you to discuss them with Heller. And of course we would welcome your views, too. As a new job, we'll be feeling our way on it, but what I have chiefly in mind is a planning role for you."

Dwight looked blank and the vice president went on. "And naturally, this promotion for you will mean a little more money — one hundred a month more, in fact."

The interview ended on that upbeat note. Dwight didn't know whether to be happy or sad.

"For heaven's sake, it's obvious. You're being bought off," cried his wife, who left no doubt about her reaction. She urged him to quit at once, but he preferred a wait-and-see response. (For an overview on the courses open in situations like this, see the fable of the "Peacock's Complaint.")

The company, its management and the individual all lose when no forthright discussion occurs with the passed-over person. The following elements should be included in the frank talk, at the very least:

1. *The reasons for another choice*. In the interview, the vice president never explained why he had picked Heller over Dwight for the job. Instead, he pretended that he had made two promotions. Thus, the officer's subterfuge proved a form of indecision as serious as Dwight's. Actually, the vice president was tempted to explain after the harangue that the accountant's indecisiveness had precluded his becoming the department manager. But the officer found himself boxed in by the fiction of the double promotion and by his own reluctance to express disagreeable truths.

2. *An opportunity for the loser to express his side*. Although the vice president should have sought and welcomed Dwight's reactions, he didn't really want them because he guessed they'd be unpleasant. Faced with a situation like this, many bosses are less than courageous and try to gloss over the situation. This is still another form of indecision that may return to haunt the offender. On the other hand, the loser should take the initiative and insist on giving his views if not invited to do so. Dwight gave his, but in a chaotic, unpersuasive form — again the result of his chronic indecision.

3. *Future prospects with the present employer for the loser*. The vice president scarcely mentioned this in his vague description of Dwight's new job — yet another form of indecision by the officer. He should have been painstakingly explicit on this subject.

4. *An offer to help the loser get a job elsewhere*. This might be with the same employer, but in another department. Or, more likely, it could be assistance elsewhere. While firing people is unpleasant, many managers haven't accepted one fact of corporate life — that in the fast-changing world of professional management, discharge is as much a

part of business life as hiring. The best way to fire someone is to do it quickly and honestly. Even if the vice president wanted Dwight to stay, however, he should have offered him the option of leaving and help in the shift. If the promotion had been genuine, he still should have made the relocation offer, with the forthright explanation that he knew the loser had hoped for the other job.

5. *A suggestion from the employer on the loser's best career course.* This is different than the offer to help get another job. Failure to win a hoped-for promotion nearly always damages a person's conception of himself. He needs reassurance, if possible, because self-doubt usually rides hard on the heels of such a defeat. By implication, the vice president gave such reassurance by apparently saying with the promotion offer, "Stay with us. You may still have a satisfactory career." He should have stated this directly — and backed up his words with action.

Events proved his implication false, of course. Dwight's new job as manager of accounting planning turned out to be the same as his old job, despite the new title and the increased salary. In fact he soon had less responsibility and authority under Heller than he had had during the interim period of no actual manager. Heller wanted no rivals and appropriated all the responsibility and authority he could find.

In his early fifties Dwight's morale and efficiency began to sag. He was kept on, however, and continued to draw a good salary and benefits for five more years. By then his authority had dwindled to nothing, and he performed as just another — and by no means outstanding — accountant among many. When he was fifty-seven, a major reorganization occurred in his company. The vice president who had procrastinated took early retirement. Heller succeeded him. One of his first acts was to let Dwight out on a disability pension because, by this time, he was suffering from physical and emotional problems.

Five years earlier, he would have had an excellent chance to land another good job. Even four years earlier when it had been obvious he would advance no further with that employer, he could and should have left for something else. By the time he was pensioned off, he was nearing a nervous breakdown. The vice president's procrastination and his own indecisiveness had cost him his physical and emotional health plus his market value as an accountant.

Modern Precept for Promotion: "Indecision slows promotions fast."

"Don't begrudge others what you can't
use yourself."

The Dog in the Manger

A Dog in the manger barked, "Nay,"
As the Cow tried to eat all day.
When the Dog fell asleep,
The Cow buried him deep,
So he nearly choked in the hay.

Aesop's Moral: "Don't begrudge others what you can't use yourself."

The Contemporary Illustration

In every business downturn, the story is the same: Many employers "discover" that they can get along with fewer employees in their administrative offices even though the amount of work remains about the same.

Earl A. took advantage of the phenomenon. He built up his little accounting empire when times were good and "did my part" when times were tighter by letting a few people go.

"It's the only way to operate," he explains privately. "If I didn't have a few extra people on board from when business was booming, I would have to let some good people go when the next edict comes along to cut back 10 per cent on my head count. It's common sense."

But Earl's superior didn't see it that way; he viewed it as hoarding. After watching Earl twice go through the cycles of expansion and contraction, he refused to okay an increase in head count during the next good phase. When he discovered that Earl had found a way to get around him by jiggering the count with tricky allocations of secretarial and professional people, he warned him. Yet, Earl persisted; so Earl found himself the first to go during the next cutback.

Although that was the specific sin the boss charged to Earl, he suspected but couldn't prove him guilty of an even more serious brand of hoarding.

Earl rarely recommended any of his people for promotion. "Needs another year or two of experience," he would say about one. "Requires close and continual supervision," he would say about another. Occasionally, he would write on somebody's performance appraisal, "Suitable for promotion in one year's time." After Earl's departure, a closer examination of the appraisal forms revealed that the same comment sometimes appeared for several years in a row for the same person.

And the fellow who supposedly needed "close and continual supervision" was found to be a self-starter under a new boss. The allegedly "inexperienced" people turned out to be veterans in several instances.

One of these proved so capable that he eventually succeeded to Earl's job. "It was the most shocking waste," said the boss who had fired Earl. "Earl had deliberately stifled him. I don't know whether he saw him as a potential rival or hid him to avoid losing him. With Earl gone, this man really blossomed."

Further delving into the machinations revealed one instance where he had strongly recommended a promotion. But this individual had failed on the higher job and left the company. The implication: Earl had recommended someone he wished to dispose of — but before the next contraction phase.

Frank L. followed a different philosophy in his corporate legal operation. When he learned of an opening in another division, he recommended his star young lawyer, Ray W., for the position — a substantial promotion.

Ray flourished in his new job and became so well-known in a few years that a larger competitor pirated him to become its general counsel. Within a year, he was president, at the age of thirty-eight. Who became his successor? Frank, who had launched him on the promotion ladder at the other company.

Did Frank feel reluctant to serve under a former employee, especially one who had defected to another employer?

"Not in the slightest," answers Frank. "When I recruited Ray out of the Yale Law School, I knew I had a comer. Within a year after he had been our division counsel, I realized his big league potential. We could never have held him, even in my old job. Maybe he would have settled for the presidency at the old shop, but he did a lot better playing it the way he did. Incidentally, I didn't do badly either."

"Incidentally," indeed.

Frank knew what he was doing in helping to push Ray upward. A good cork in water will always rise to the top. Only if it allows itself to be pushed under again and again, will it eventually grow waterlogged and stay at the bottom. Frank knew that Ray would swim well in the corporate currents and wouldn't sink, no matter what Frank might do.

Others do go to the bottom, however, and stay there. Remember

Ralph, the victim of a reorganization in "Belling the Cat"? He narrowly avoided such a fate by finding a new job outside the company.

But Tom in that same fable allowed himself to go under. Walt conned young Tom into helping him with his career — with Walt playing the role of a particularly virulent "Dog in the Manger," because he ruined Tom's progress in the attempt.

So, keep on guard about seeming "friends" apparently willing to help you in your career. They may turn out to be less than man's best friend.

On the other hand, some people are nice, as was the acquaintance who helped Ed. J. become a vice president's statistical analyst in "Belling the Cat."

Of all the Dog-in-the-Manger problems, probably the most pernicious involves little more than pure spite.

Belle Y. had the characteristic in abundance. In an upstate New York consolidated school system, she had served a principal as secretary for twenty-two years. Privately, she considered herself as the actual principal; in practice she probably came close to her own assessment of her role. Her boss had grown lazy in the job and relied on her increasingly.

Sally T., on her first teaching assignment as science teacher for the sixth grade, particularly annoyed Belle. She tried unsuccessfully to fix the paper jams in the Xerox machine and asked Belle to remedy the matter. Sally had a little trouble with class discipline and sent offenders to the principal's office. Belle resented their presence while they waited for him. Sally was somewhat slap-dash in submitting the various reports that Belle had the responsibility for collecting.

Furthermore, many of the pupils adored the gentle Sally, but none of them adored Belle. So, Belle began a campaign against Sally. Unfortunately, it worked because the principal recommended that Sally's contract not be renewed for the next year.

Modern Precept for Promotion: "Champion others' ambitions — if you don't hold them yourself."

"Greed is sometimes caught by its
own bait."

The Dog and the Shadow

To pond's bridge came a dog with his bone.
There in the water his image shone.
To him the mirrored meat
Looked tastier to eat.
When he snapped, his own bone sank like stone.

Aesop's Moral: "Greed is sometimes caught by its own bait."

The Contemporary Illustration

Wesley C. groped for the ringing telephone beside his bed.

"Yes." He had to clear his throat to pronounce even the simple syllable.

"Harshman of the *News*," came the voice on the line. "Sorry to wake you at this hour, but we've just got wind of a development in welfare that we'd like you to comment on."

Wes grimaced as he squinted at his bedside clock radio. Six-thirty — an hour before he normally got up. He cleared his throat again, but muffled the sound in the blankets before he spoke.

"No trouble at all, Jim. What's the problem?" He had met Harshman only once in person and had spoken to him on the phone a few times. But he knew him as the author of many by-lined articles for the city's largest newspaper, including a recent series uncomplimentary to his boss, the commissioner. Wes had publicly deplored them, but privately he had liked them because they might further his own ambitions.

"We understand you people in the Welfare Department," the reporter said, "are going to start a new system of validation of welfare clients that aims at cutting relief roles by 10 per cent or more."

Wes managed a fair imitation of a jovial chuckle. "Jim, I have to hand it to you guys. You fellows must have some sources."

"Well, what's the score?"

"Jim, you're putting me on the spot. You must know I can't comment on that yet." Now thoroughly awake, Wes was in more of a spot than Harshman may have realized. Wes knew nothing about any fresh validation scheme. But all kinds of proposals had been floating throughout the department for months. Anything could happen, but the distressing aspect was that he had not been privy to any new development. That upset him. Although validation proposals didn't originate in his shop, any outsider would expect him to have inside information as one of three assistant commissioners for welfare. Wes felt gratified that Harshman had called him, especially because he had had little luck with the *News* thus far. Also because his predecessor had apparently known an inside track to the paper, he wished to exploit this opening.

"Does this rumor hold up?" Harshman asked brusquely.

"We've considered dozens of different validation schemes recently."

"This one's known as Proposal G."

Wes tightened his grip on the phone receiver. He had never heard of Proposal G, or F for that matter. "Honestly now, Jim, I'd like to help you, but I can't at this time. As the code name implies, it's still in proposal form. Nothing is concrete yet."

Harshman's voice took on a rasp of impatience. "Let's not play with words. You know and I know that this thing has gone beyond the proposal stage, even if it's still called that. Can you or can you not confirm this and give me some details?"

"I can tell you this," said Wes, stalling as best he could. "We hope to announce something very soon, but we're not ready yet."

"Hell, that's meaningless." Now Harshman openly voiced his disgust.

Wes thought hard. Harshman could help him in his climb to the top in the welfare agency. The *News* had been attacking the commissioner almost every week editorially for nearly a year. The paper could prove valuable in supporting him, Wes, for the job if he recruited allies from its staff like Harshman. He had already received favorable notice in interviews by reporters from the city's two other newspapers.

At twenty-nine, he was by far the youngest assistant commissioner in any of the city's score of agencies. His meteoric rise in only four years as a civil servant resulted from a combination of luck, ability and another quality that the mayor referred to when he said that Wes "had more brass than a burglar."

That characteristic had caught His Honor's attention three and a half years earlier. The mayor had the political astuteness already to have won the city's top job three times. But the fourth election loomed only a year ahead, and His Honor recognized that his administration had lost its image of youth after eleven years in office. So he was looking for fresh blood when Wes brassily caught his attention.

With his new master's degree in public health administration, Wes had first joined the Health Department; but in less than six months he had seen that only a dim future lay before him in that backwater. The instrument that had whirled him into the mayor's orbit was a proposal to merge Health into Welfare in the interests of efficiency and common sense. He had ignored all protocol by mailing a well-argued document directly to the mayor, who had been impressed by the paper and amused by its author's audacity. While the merger had come to nothing, the mayor had met Wes, shrewdly recognized how the young man might help the mayoral image, and moved him over to Welfare in a much higher post than he had held at Health.

The shift had exhilarated Wes. He had the intelligence to sense the reasons underlying it and exploited them shamelessly.

In his first Welfare post as assistant director of public relations, he used his entree to the mayor to persuade him to participate in a wide-ranging interview on welfare over a local television station's Sunday afternoon show, "Today's Issues." The welfare commissioner was miffed, but the mayor was delighted. Soon, with the uncanny instinct of their kind, most of the media representatives got in touch with Wes rather than the agency's PR director, Jones, when they wanted information. Both the commissioner and the director became justifiably enraged when Wes emerged as the spokesman on welfare in a series run by one of the city papers, which neither of his superiors had known was planned.

The PR director rashly offered his resignation to the commissioner who had no intention of accepting it until the mayor intervened. Mysteriously, His Honor knew of the resignation and advised the commissioner to accept it and promote Wes to the job. When the commissioner got this word, he swallowed his own indignation and accepted both the resignation and Wes's promotion. The commissioner owed his job to the mayor.

Wes had deliberately goaded the PR head into the action. Furthermore, Jones's twenty-year-old secretary had been carefully cultivated, so Wes knew every move he made. The rising civil servant told the mayor of the impending resignation and of his wish for the job.

Wes had helped win the mayor's re-election in several ways — as a publicity consultant on his campaign staff and, more importantly, as the organizer for "voluntary" campaign donations from Welfare Department employees. As a reward for his aid, the mayor forced a "reorganization" of the Welfare Department after his re-election, creating a new third assistant commissioner, Wes, who continued to head up public relations plus a few other odds and ends to make the change appear legitimate.

Yet since the election and the promotion, Wes's fortunes had ebbed because His Honor's political star had slipped. The mayor had been hurt politically by a bus strike and slowdowns by police and firemen. The administration had begun levying an unpopular city income tax, and the *News* continued an unrelenting attack on the welfare system.

"Well, what about it?" rasped Harshman.

Wes realized with a start that he had remained silent for nearly a minute as he thought of ways he might recoup his fortunes with the help of the reporter and his paper. "Sorry, Jim. I was trying to mull over in my mind the best way I could help you and not get the whole department in hot water. Can you hold off on this thing for twenty-four hours? Then I can give you some inside stuff."

Wes was really stalling some more because he was completely in the dark about Proposal G. Harshman apparently suspected as much because he objected.

"But it will be exclusive to you, Jim." Wes wheedled and pleaded, but the reporter adamantly held out for a statement confirming or denying. Afraid both of appearing stupid and of alienating Harshman, Wes said, "Okay, you can confirm it but don't quote me or name me at this time. Later, yes, twenty-four hours from now." Harshman agreed to that and at last hung up.

Wes stormed into the commissioner's office ten minutes after arriving for work that morning.

"Am I running PR or not?" he gritted as he angrily reported the phone conversation earlier. "What in hell is Proposal G, and why haven't I been filled in on it?"

"Proposal G?" The commissioner turned his hand palm up. He rarely wasted energy, physical or emotional. "Never heard of it."

"Come on, damn it. Don't hand me that. You're holding out on me again — just like in that welfare chiselling case last month."

The commissioner smiled like a teacher reproving a backward pupil. "Wes, we've been round and round on that chiselling thing. You weren't informed because of a slipup in the paper work. You know that."

"Paper work slipup, my ass. You didn't choose to tell me because you were trying to cover up and hoped the mayor wouldn't learn of it."

The commissioner continued the smile that rarely left him — even in the face of abuse from a greedily ambitious youngster or disagreeable instructions from his boss, the mayor. "You've called me a liar before. I've told you before that I don't like it. And I'll tell you again. I am not a liar and I don't like to be called one."

"What is Proposal G?" Wes enunciated each word as though he were talking to someone hard of hearing.

"Pride of place has its disadvantages."

The Fir and the Bramble

The Fir Tree looked down on the Bramble.
"Poor thing — all it can do is scramble."
But when cut from its hill,
Proud Fir went to a mill,
While Bramble continued to ramble.

Aesop's Moral: "Pride of place has its disadvantages."

The Contemporary Illustration

Pamela U. had kept her eye on the boss's office all day. Seldom had she seen such coming and going. Half the lawyers on Alpha International's legal staff must have visited Ned just that morning. And when someone had not occupied him in person, the associate general counsel had been on the phone.

Pam grew more certain that something exceptional had happened. Ned's secretary — inhibited bitch! — had simply shrugged when Pam had tried to pump her. As the youngest member of what some people derisively called the Alpha International Bar Association and only a year off the training program for company lawyers, she didn't feel she could probe too deeply. But Ned would tell her if she could ever get in to see him!

She had mixed attitudes toward what she knew was a "special" relationship with her boss.

"Maybe he wants to go to bed with me," she had confided to her girl friend and roommate one night after a dinner date with him. "But he's never said so right out. And he's a gentleman. No pawing. Not even a kiss. Nothing suggestive."

"Well for heaven's sake! What d'ya talk about?"

"Ned." Pam had giggled.

"My God, what a bore he must be!"

"Funny thing, but he isn't. He really talks about his philosophy of life and business and only about himself indirectly."

Pam knew that she served as his sounding board. She was flattered that he asked her — a virtual neophyte's — opinion on office matters.

At first, he had merely sought her appraisal of the relative merits of various secretaries. Gradually, he had given her the task of assigning some of the more routine chores among the various junior legal staff members.

"You're my assignments editor," he had said. Indeed, the title proved apt because most of the work she had and the other juniors did were brief summaries on judicial decisions that might affect Alpha International. Pam drew the Swedish, Dutch and German decisions because of her aptitude for those languages. Indeed, the language knack had landed her the job with Ned whose legal responsibilities included Alpha's overseas activities. The company's other associate general counsel had jurisdiction over domestic legal matters involving the company.

Finally, Ned seemed free, so Pam slipped in. "What on earth's going on?"

He smiled and looked at his watch. "I'll tell you all about it at dinner. Meet you at Roma's at seven. OK?"

She had gone home to her apartment to change, so had arrived at Roma's a little late. He waved aside her apologies.

"It gave me time to unwind with a drink. It's been quite a day. When I saw you coming in I ordered a martini for you. Double."

"Ned! You know that could put me on my ear."

"We've got something to celebrate. Old Man Hogan has resigned, but just between you and me he was fired over that U.S. antitrust mess the domestic boys got us into."

She had only met Hogan, the vice president and general counsel, once when she had gone on the training program and had had nothing to do with him since, even though he headed Alpha's entire legal operation.

"Oh, Ned, then you're going to succeed him!"

Ned burst into laughter. "Never, my dear, would I take that job. Not even for $100,000 a year, which was what they were paying the son of a gun. No, that guy has given me more trouble than an old maid. That's why I'm bidding him such a fond farewell. Besides, my real reason for celebrating is . . ." Ned took a reflective sip from his Scotch. ". . . *my* man will be the new vice president. Stevens, the legal counsel for the Omega Division. You don't know him, but you'll like him. He's a great guy."

"Ned, I don't get it. Why don't you want the vice presidency?"

"Because the job is trouble. It's a lightning rod and takes all the voltage, while we stay safe and snug out of harm's way. Let the Hogans

and Stevenses of this world have their pride of position. I want the real power — behind the throne. And I'll have it with Stevens to a degree I never could with old Hogan."

She frowned into her martini. "Yes, but what if it doesn't work out? What if he wants his own people in the top jobs like yours?"

"Honey, trust Uncle Ned." She was mulling over his use of a term of endearment for the second time that evening, in contrast to all their other dates when he had never used any. So she missed some of his comments and picked up as he was saying, ". . . I've lasted out three vice presidents in the past fifteen years. I've moved up the ladder in title or money with every one, and I'm going to do the same with Stevens."

"How much higher can you go without becoming vice president?"

"Behind the scenes, that's where, out of harm's way for the time being. This antitrust business isn't over yet, not by a long shot. Anybody that's involved with it, even after the fact like now, is likely to get tarred with the thing. No, my darling, the international wing is a good shelter for now."

Three times, she thought. And a divorced man eighteen years older!

"Just you see," he was saying. "I'll have Stevens eating out of my hand. He called me twice today, and he wants a session with me first thing on Monday when he arrives in town."

That night when Ned took her home, there was no doubt what he wanted. She held him at bay with the excuse (true) that her roommate was home and that she didn't like going to a motel or hotel. As consolation prize, she awarded him their first kiss.

She feared she would have amorous trouble with Ned, but he was preoccupied with briefing Stevens. It turned out that the new vice president was a bachelor, so Pam suggested a double date with her roommate the next time Ned asked her out for dinner. The evening proved so successful that it evolved into a weekly pattern.

Almost a year later, Pam expressed surprise when Ned objected to a double date.

"I never see you alone anymore," he complained. "And frankly I'm getting a little tired of these small-hour 'rap' sessions back at your apartment."

"But Ned, you don't stay for them half the time."

"You're so right! I've got to get my sleep. I don't know how Stevens can take it."

"He seems to enjoy them."

So, the double dates gradually ceased. Ned grew increasingly critical of Stevens. "The guy's a lousy judge of people," he said one evening at

Roma's. "I told him Ames was a poor choice as associate counsel on the domestic side. Granger should have gotten the job, but Stevens wouldn't hear of it."

When the vice president insisted that Pam go to Sweden to handle a legal matter for Alpha, Ned scarcely bothered to hide his disapproval from Pam.

"But Ned, I'm the only one in the office who can speak Swedish."

"All Swedish lawyers know English. You don't need to savvy the language."

"Yes, but it helps to speak it, and I'm thrilled to be going."

Ned just grunted.

Almost three years had passed since the time of the new vice president's arrival. Ned and Pam still saw each other socially, but not as often as formerly. One evening at Roma's, he blurted out:

"Pam, I'm leaving Alpha."

She nodded.

"You don't seem very surprised."

"I know you've been more and more unhappy."

"That's putting it mildly. Frankly, Stevens has been a bitter disappointment to me."

"Have you got anything else lined up?" Pam asked.

"Oh yes." He named a firm specializing in international law that he would be joining.

"I'm so glad, Ned. I think it would be better for you."

"How do you mean?"

"Well, away from all the office politics at Alpha. All this — well this manipulating that you like to do."

"Manipulating? That's a word Stevens used this afternoon. He accused me of trying to do it."

Pam looked into her drink. "He doesn't like it, I know."

Ned took a reflective swallow. "Well, a lot of manipulating I've been doing. As my successor, he nixed Longley, who was my candidate. I don't even know who it will be. He refused to say."

"I asked him not to tell, Ned. I'm going to succeed you."

Modern Precept for Promotion: "Pride goes before the fall."

"Pleasure bought with pain, hurts."

The Flies and the Honey

The flies found the honey spilled and sweet.
They gorged with gusto, although not neat.
But when they had their fill
And tried to leave the sill,
Sticky goo had trapped them by their feet.

Aesop's Moral: "Pleasure bought with pain, hurts."

The Contemporary Illustration

Karen F. watched the stray cloud slide by in the bright blue Jamaican sky. Although she had been vacationing for two weeks on this Caribbean island, she still couldn't believe this tropical paradise — so warm, so languid, so . . . sweet. With bitter regret, she realized she would have to leave in two days — back to the snow and cold of upstate New York in March, back to her unruly sixth graders.

She shook her head as if she could shake off the thought. She had the urge to talk to someone and rose from her beach chair beside the villa's private pool and went looking for a companion. In her bedroom, Betty was fast asleep. In the other bedroom the other two girls who had come down to share this house with her also slept in the time-honored siesta of the tropics. Strange how quickly northerners slipped into these languid habits! Except herself today.

Yet she too had been taking the siesta until now. Never had she regretted the end of a vacation as she had this one. She and her sister, Betty, had planned it for two years — their first junket outside the United States. It had been perfect. They had even met four darling boys in a neighboring villa and had spent nearly every evening with them.

The villas had rented for periods of four weeks only, so they had had to take this place for that time, despite the fact that none of the girls had four weeks' vacation. Betty, the lucky stiff, got three weeks from her lawyer boss and had arranged to take an additional week without pay. The other two girls had made similar arrangements with their industrial employers.

Karen could finagle only three weeks away from school by dint of the two weeks' Easter vacation, Good Friday and crafty use of sick leave for four days before Good Friday. She had planned to fly back home a week ahead of the other three. During the planning for this outing, she had thought this would be no problem, and she had welcomed the lower rental that she would have to pay. But now she felt like a child on Christmas afternoon. All the fun was over.

Suddenly she shrieked. Hands had come over her eyes. She squirmed around. Her anger and fright turned to relief. "Stevie, you nut, you startled me." The boy at the neighboring villa, the one she had paired off with most frequently, stood grinning at her.

"Sorry, Karen, but I just had a great idea and came right over to tell you about it."

"Good, I need a great idea now."

He sat at the end of her deck chair, tanned and blond. She felt a shiver of delight every time she looked at him. She made no effort to pull away as his hand rested casually on her left knee. When he had tried this sort of thing before, she had resisted. The other girls, all older than she, had kidded her about her prudishness, even Betty. "For heaven's sake, unwind, Karen," she had urged. "A little kiss won't hurt anything. You might even enjoy it. You're acting like an old-maid schoolteacher of forty-two not twenty-four."

"What I suggest is this," Steve was continuing. "Let's ask that doctor who's in the pink villa over on Crest Drive to agree to sign a cable to your school superintendent, saying you are sick, can't return — food poisoning or something. Then you could stay for another week."

"Oh, he'd never do a thing like that." Karen frowned.

"Sure he would. The old coot gives you the eye every time he thinks his wife's not looking."

"But the school superintendent might catch him out when he gets back to the states."

"He'd never check. Doc practices in New York City. You're two hundred miles from there."

"I've already worked that sick dodge during the four days before good Friday." She tried not to watch as his hand crept further up her leg.

"So much the better. You've had a relapse." Steve reached into a pocket with a free hand, pulled out a folded piece of paper and shook it open. "I've already got a draft of a cable for you."

The cable read: "Regret Karen Folger suffering from intestinal gastritis. Too ill to travel. Will advise when she can return." The cable bore the name of Martin S. Carnaby, M.D., the vacationing doctor.

"He'll never agree to this," protested Karen.

"Sure he will. Just bat those pretty blue eyes at him tonight at cocktails." Steve smiled at her puzzlement. "We're having a party tonight. He's invited and so are you."

As she stared in surprise and pleasure, he quickly kissed her for the first time.

To cover her confusion, she stammered, "I'll . . . I'll have to talk to Betty."

"Oh come on. You're a big girl now. Besides you have talked it over — with me."

Nevertheless, Karen did talk it over with Betty — both as an excuse to forestall any further intimacies with Steve and because she genuinely wanted her advice.

When her older sister had awakened enough to grasp the problem, she was as positive as usual. "Of course, you should try it. What can you lose?"

"My job," wailed Karen.

"So what? There are other teaching jobs — and certainly better ones than that detention home you're stuck in. If you've told me once, you've told me a thousand times how you hate it."

So, Karen agreed to approach Dr. Carnaby. It all went so smoothly and agreeably that she was left almost speechless. The doctor thought it a huge joke. Not only did he agree to have his name on the cable, but he scribbled out a note on a prescription pad to the same effect, for use when she faced the school superintendent again. A phone call also quickly got her new plane reservations for one week later.

The next week passed in a feverish gaiety that Karen had never known before. When Steve made a determined effort to seduce her, she resisted the first time, but again consulted with Betty.

"Sweetheart," she laughed, "how did I ever get such an inhibited gal for a sister? It's up to you, of course, but the other three of us have been having it with the other boys right along. Steve wants it so bad from you he's ready to explode."

Under her tan, Karen flushed. "You mean you've been sleeping with Eddie?"

Betty laughed. "How Victorian you are, darling. I've been screwing with him. Very little sleeping.'"

So, Karen took more advice on contraception from Betty and that evening lost her virginity to Steve.

Just before she and the other girls were to leave, she stayed with Steve all night for the first time.

"When are we going to see each other again, honey?" she asked during one lull in their activity.

"Gosh, sweetheart, that's going to be a problem, with me in Atlanta and you in the wilds of New York State."

"Couldn't you come up this summer?"

"I sure hope so, sugar, but I've pretty much blown my vacation for the year on this blast."

"Well, a weekend maybe?"

"Sure, I'll write you."

The boys were going to Miami from Montego Bay later on the next day. So, they didn't accompany the girls who had to leave for New York City on an earlier flight.

The goodbyes were muted all around, and Karen muttered later on the long taxi trip to Montego, "They could at least have offered to drive us over."

Betty laughed. "Are you kidding? We'll never see them again. They've got their southern belles stashed away in Atlanta."

On the plane trip back, Karen couldn't help crying quietly in her window seat.

"For God's sake, pull yourself together," Betty hissed. "This isn't the end of the world. We'll have other vacations and other men."

Karen's dispiritedness wasn't improved by Superintendent Kupper's reception as she arrived back at school one week late.

"Yes, I got your cable," he acknowledged frostily. "I am forced to dock you for a week's pay. You're lucky I don't also withhold for the four days before Easter."

"But Mr. Kupper, I was ill. Here's a note from Dr. Carnaby."

The superintendent looked at the scrawled words on the prescription blank. "Who is this Carnaby? Never heard of him."

She explained the circumstances, while Kupper jotted down names and other notes.

A week later she was called in again to see Kupper. Without preamble, he said, "I'm sorry to say, Miss Folger, that we will be unable to renew your contract next year. I'm telling you now so that you can begin making other plans."

"Is this because of my Easter vacation illness?"

"Lack of discipline is the main problem with you."

"But Mr. Kupper, this is unfair. I have the worst troublemakers in the sixth grade. The other teachers have told me so."

"It's not only disciplinary problems in the classroom, Miss Folger. I don't believe you discipline yourself well."

"You mean my Easter absence? I was sick."

"I called this Dr. Carnaby. I'm not satisfied with his account. He seemed to take the whole affair as a big joke."

Modern Precept for Promotion: "Self-discipline is a hard, but sure road to job success."

"Never trust a flatterer."

The Fox and the Crow

Said sly Fox to Crow with the cheese,
"Sing a sweet song for me, now, please,"
So this Crow, being vain,
Cawed a short, hoarse refrain —
And dropped the cheese for Fox to seize.

Aesop's Moral: "Never trust a flatterer."

The Contemporary Illustration

"Flattery will get you everywhere," said Mae West in one of her immortal lines — a wry twist to the older saw, "Flattery will get you nowhere." Unfortunately, Mae West may have come closer to the truth than the long forgotten author of the original adage.

Many people can't distinguish between flattery and praise. Flattery, says the dictionary, is insincere praise, while praise is honest commendation. Ben K. could seldom tell the difference. He had doubts about the offer to become vice president of marketing for one of the lesser known banks in his city because the institution had a reputation for links with crime. The flattery of a vice presidency, which he had never achieved at the large bank that had employed him for eighteen years, swayed him partially to accept the offer.

A related but more subtle brand of flattery took him the rest of the way along the road to a promotion.

"You, the son of the great Ben K., Sr., deserve a vice presidency," the head of the little known bank told him. That, of course, matched Ben K., Jr.'s sentiments exactly. His father had been the chairman and chief executive officer of the large bank until his death, but Ben had never even made the vice presidential level.

Yet young Ben had never fully examined the corollary to the claim that he allegedly deserved a vice presidency. The prospective new employer required his name, his aura of respectability. Ben soon learned that the bank needed that more than he needed the title. His new employer, he discovered to his horror, did indeed have dubious practices — if not illegal at least unethical. He resigned in six months, to return to his first employer, supposedly a wiser if sadder man.

So, the first challenge in dealing with approval is to determine whether it's sincere. If sincere, accept it happily. If not, take care.

Some signs of insincere approval:

- When it's overly effusive.
- When it's at least partly undeserved.
- When it embarrasses you.
- When it puzzles you.
- When it comes frequently.

Heed, particularly, this last signal because flattery is common and true praise is rare. A perceptive person in an employer-employee relationship doesn't praise often. He knows that praise really constitutes an evaluation. And people often automatically flinch at evaluations, even when they're favorable, because next time the evaluation may hurt. Positive evaluation also may bring discomfort because it reminds the recipient that the person doing the praising sits in judgment upon him — a disquieting reminder.

Expressed approval may also be neither sincere nor insincere; it may be little more than a social lubricant. When the boss says, "nice job," or something similar, he usually means, "I'm glad you got that done on time," or "I don't have to worry about this anymore," or merely, "Thank you." To take such remarks as anything but social gestures would be ridiculous.

Yet some people read into this verbiage unwarranted meanings that have led to pathetic contretemps. Lorraine V. didn't become manager of the computer programming staff, so she blurted out to the boss who had not chosen her, "I guess all your praise was just flattery!"

Baffled, he probed further because he thought he had almost never expressed approval to her. In fact, he held her in rather low regard and had never remotely considered her for managership. It turned out that she had hoarded in her mind all his "nice job" comments, burnishing them into high praise and beguiling herself into a belief that the boss admired her abilities.

The lesson of Lorraine is this: You are vulnerable to flattery if you hunger too much for praise. Similarly, the lesson of Ben is: You are vulnerable to flattery if you hunger too much for status.

Flattery will victimize you, also, if you don't see the true motives behind expressions of approval. Of course the motive may be sincerely commendatory. Fine, but look first at a few less pleasant possibilities.

Does the person expressing approval want you to do something that serves his interests more than yours? If so, that's flattery. Ben learned to his sorrow that he had listened more to flattery than to praise.

Does the person expressing approval want you sidelined or compla-cent during a particularly competitive job situation? If so, that's flattery. Nora D., a music teacher in a New Jersey public system, ran into that situation. Nora wished to move to the top job, teacher of chorus in the high school, upon the retirement of the man who held the position.

She called upon him to seek his recommendation.

"My dear," he said. "I'm really touched that you came to ask my advice. Of course, you are the prime candidate. You are doing wonders with the elementary children. I can see the difference in their training now that the first ones that had you have reached me. I envy you in your position. You can take the children when they're young, their voices unspoiled and really start them off right. It must bring great satisfaction to you."

When Nora had first come to the high school choral director, she hadn't felt any great satisfaction in teaching unspoiled voices. After an hour's conversation, she really did believe for a while that she held the best music job in the school system, even though she formerly had wanted a promotion. She eased off in her efforts to get the job, and it went to the junior high school music teacher.

She learned later that the winner in the job sweepstakes had been the choice all along of the man retiring. He had flattered her into with-drawing from the competition.

Does the person expressing approval want the job you now hold? If so, that's flattery and a special-case application of the first two motives.

The music teacher at the junior high school had won the senior music director's approval because he had cleverly flattered the older man.

"We're going to miss you," he would tell him. "We'll need you as a consultant until we make up for the loss. The school board should pay you some sort of consulting fee."

That thought had occurred to the man retiring, too, and he therefore looked kindly on his junior. On the other hand, Nora believed the senior man had become little more than a time-server at the school. She could never have brought herself to flatter him.

Once you recognize expressed approval as flattery, you have already applied some of the medicine needed to deal with the malady. For the rest of the treatment, the most effective remedy is benign neglect.

Jeanne T., an attractive librarian for a pharmaceutical firm, treated all the compliments as badinage. She couldn't always be certain whether she was hearing praise or flattery, but she played safe and reacted to it all with light banter. Even the men who praised her didn't take offense because they enjoyed the byplay. When she eventually became the head librarian, her promotion met almost universal commendation. She had skirted all the dangers that can come from flattery and had offended no one who had actually praised her.

Another good reaction to flattery is to return the insincere praise. Nora would have been wiser to return the fulsome compliments to the senior music man. That course might at least have stopped him in his con job on her and she would not have been lulled into such dangerous complacency. However, she did not at first recognize the flattery for what it was, so she couldn't counterattack.

Modern Precept for Promotion: "To win promotions, learn to distinguish between flattery and praise."

"Its easy to scorn what you can't get."

The Fox and the Grapes

The Fox wanted grapes in a bower.
He jumped and he jumped for an hour.
The vines were high, yet near,
So Fox said with a sneer,
"The grapes are no good; they're sour."

Aesop's Moral: "Its easy to scorn what you can't get."

The Contemporary Illustration

Some 35 per cent of managers answering a recent survey said they would consider joining a union. Respondents to an American Management Association quiz of more than a thousand managers said that they consider themselves blocked in a promotion, with no one they can appeal to about the problem . . . while unionized employees at least can grieve to their union stewards if they don't get better jobs.

Have a third of those managers responding to the survey appraised their own abilities realistically? Some undoubtedly have and deserve a promotion. What should they do? The best advice: Leave for better opportunities before sour-grapes attitudes corrode their careers and lives. But what if leaving is impractical? The next best advice: At least minimize the danger of sour grapes as much as possible by methods I'll discuss soon.

Yet, what if it's not open-and-shut that some of those managers did deserve promotion? What should they do? They should ask themselves questions such as these: Have I realistically examined the reasons I didn't get promoted? Am I unreasonably impatient, not deserving a promotion now? Do my personal, professional or social attitudes turn my superiors off?

On this attitudinal aspect, consider the case of Jay D. As a writer of product publicity, he was ambitious and his wife expensive. When he could not get a better paying job with his employer, a maker of cutting tools, he found one as assistant manager of product promotion with a competitor.

Jay soon encountered difficulties. He goofed in his assignment to help with a company exhibit at a trade show. He was embarrassed when it became obvious that he did not know as much as he had claimed about the esoterica of mailing lists. Even worse, Jay resumed a bad habit that had limited his advancement with his previous employer. He began knocking his boss when the going got rough, suggesting too freely that the whole trade show had been poorly planned and that direct mail should not be used to sell cutting tools.

Inevitably, such comments circulated back to the boss. They became a factor in his decision to fire Jay only six months after he had hired him.

If Jay had kept his mouth shut, he might have weathered the storm because his errors could have been laid to inexperience or misunderstanding. As it was, he had to leave town to find a new publicity job. However, his wife didn't follow him.

Or take the attitudinal problems of Bob I. As a graduate of Harvard Business School, he at first climbed the pyramid rapidly with a large electronics company — until he became a plant manager. In that position, he encountered for the first time some of the grimier aspects of running a factory—the contentious union representatives, the pressure for higher productivity, and even the boss talks at 6:30 A.M. to the third shift made sullen at being prevented from going home a half-hour early as usual.

He let his unhappiness become known. When he asked for a transfer to manage a new company project, his request was refused because top management now saw him as "lacking enthusiasm."

Then Bob caught the sour-grapes syndrome seriously. He openly criticized the new project as ill-conceived. When it proved highly successful, Bob looked like a fool.

He subsequently left the corporate world — because it was "impossible" — for a minor administrative post in a midwestern university. He never rose far there either when he saw fit to refuse one critical promotion into a fund-raising post because he considered it a booby trap set by rivals to lure him into failure.

Sour grapes became a mental habit with Bob. It ruined a promising career. How can you avoid such a pernicious habit? Largely by recognizing its dangers, using all the mental discipline at your command to keep thinking positively, and never discussing your grievances with overly sympathetic friends. Bob's uncritically loyal wife unwittingly contributed to his downfall. She suffered with him at his every setback, providing no counterbalance to him. Instead, she reinforced his negative attitudes and precipitated his fall.

Jack M. was more fortunate. He had a managership thrust upon him in the accounting department. His boss, all smiles and joviality, called him into his office one day.

"Jack, you've been doing a great job. As you may know, Ed will be retiring in two months. I want you to take over in accounts receivable. You'll have Ed's four fellows reporting to you, and there will be $100 a month more in the pay check, too. I guess you can use that, eh?"

Jack faced a dilemma. Of course, he could use the added money. But, he couldn't very well explain that he left his former job with a smaller firm because he had hated his management job there. He had given as an excuse for leaving the half-truth that he had wanted experience in a bigger, more diversified company.

So for the moment Jack temporized and pretended delight at the promotion. In recounting the episode to his wife, he half-persuaded himself to try managing again as he emphasized the added income and rationalized that "you can't turn down promotions because you'll never get another if you do."

Indeed, it is difficult to refuse a promotion, especially if the person handing it out needs to fill the job. An added problem lies in the fact that most big promotions do involve managerships. The promotional channels through the route of individual contributorship are limited, except in large organizations.

In Jack's case, his wife brought him back to earth. She reminded him of his unhappiness when he had been a manager before. He decided to refuse the new job. The boss showed more understanding than Jack had expected. In the months that followed Jack had moments of doubt about his wisdom, but he kept those doubts to himself and never yielded to the temptation to resort to sour grapes in words or, even more importantly, in attitudes.

A year later there was an opening for a statistical analyst in one of the company's divisions. It involved individual contributing, not managing, and a raise comparable to that originally offered to manage the accounts receivable operation.

An objective, realistic examination of the reasons for the failure to win a promotion can forestall sour grapes. But you have to guard against your own rationalizations that sometimes can be so devilishly ingenious that they will fool the most perceptive, including yourself.

Ruth A. was a whiz in personnel work. She became the first female personnel manager in her company. She won a promotion to a staff job in headquarters but didn't do as well. Furthermore, her salty language and "just one of the boys" manner which had amused her associates at the plant level did not intrigue the more formal types in headquarters. When her boss suggested that "you might be happier in the field," she refused to return. After she failed to get another promotion, she filed a claim of sex discrimination with state and federal agencies.

She became a Women's Lib advocate, steadily escalating her stridency. Her complaints, lawsuits and causes took up so much of her time that she retired early at fifty-five, abandoning a promising and self-fulfilling career in personnel. She was far less happy as a crusader than she had been as a manager in personnel. Although she strongly denied the charge of sour grapes, many believe that she camouflaged, at least to herself, her own limitations by adopting alleged sex discrimination as an explanation for her failure to win promotions.

Ruth refused to consider the possibility that she didn't deserve a promotion. Have you examined that proposition for your own case? Admittedly, such self-analysis is difficult. Step outside yourself temporarily. Look at the situation as if a friend, rather than you, faced the predicament.

For example, if Jay had mustered such objectivity and put the pressures from his wife in proper perspective, he might have seen that he was being unreasonably impatient in his ambition. Events certainly proved that he would have profited more by staying in his first job.

It takes maturity and lack of pretense to admit that you don't deserve a promotion. Jack had those qualities sufficiently to refuse the first better job opportunity and to wait patiently for the more appropriate second offer.

Modern Precept for Promotion: "Chances for real promotion improve when you avoid sour-grapes attitudes."

"Imaginary fears are the worst."

The Frightened Lion

Small Frog by his pool went "croak."
A Lion, coming up to soak,
Leaped far back in alarm,
Thinking only of harm,
As the Frog with laughter did choke.

Aesop's Moral: "Imaginary fears are the worst."

The Contemporary Illustration

Ted Q. performed well as a salesman for business forms and supplies, but fears often dogged him.

On the one hand, he felt he should rise into the administrative side of sales, but he had never asked for such a move. With some reason, he believed he could not achieve that ambition because his employer valued him too highly "on the line." At other times, he felt he lacked talent for anything but "peddling." Once or twice a year when he lost a good sale, he fought fits of depression when he believed he could not succeed even in selling.

When his firm hired new salesmen, he viewed them as rivals even though he knew the ridiculousness of that fear. As the perennial top salesman for his company, he had had no real rivals in years. He suffered vague fears occasionally that the new salesmen or others were "out to get him." Although he knew in his mind that such feelings were irrational, he nevertheless had them.

Is Ted some kind of nut? Perhaps. But if he is, a lot of other Americans are, too. One in eight Americans will suffer a bout of depression serious enough to need psychiatric help during his lifetime. According to the National Institute of Mental Health, 125,000 Americans are hospitalized each year with depression, while another 200,000 are treated on psychiatrists' couches or in physicians' offices. Another 4 million to 8 million need help but don't know it. Ted fell within this last group.

Depression has been diagnosed by physicians at least since Hippocrates. The disorder has afflicted many notable figures in history. Churchill wrote about the "black dog" that hounded him throughout life and immobilized him during his final years. Abraham Lincoln also suffered from melancholia. The artist, Vincent van Gogh, cut off his ear during a fit of despair.

Depression has victimized enough notable people to suggest to some psychiatrists that sensitive, creative and overachieving persons are peculiarly susceptible to it. Studies now going on among those patronizing free psychiatric clinics indicate that depression knows no economic boundaries. It can hit anybody.

Depression's irony lies in the fact that it does drive some people to prodigious effort and achievement. When Ted suffered his periodic fears about competition from fancied rivals, he usually chalked up his best sales performances. Yet depression also brought on apathy in other areas for him. He could not bring himself to ask for an administrative sales job. While he probably could not have won such a position with his own employer, he had had numerous offers over the years from competitive companies where he could have virtually written his own job specifications. In the face of each opportunity, he procrastinated until the chance slipped away. In turn, these episodes usually precipitated other bouts of depression.

Everyone has highs and lows in mood, and grief over a serious loss is normal. However, when the moods swing in an exaggerated way and when grief lasts for months or years, a person suffers from depression.

Still, the true nature of the illness eludes psychiatric and psychological investigators. Does it arise from outside stress or faulty body chemistry — or from a combination of both? During depression, a victim experiences apathy, lack of self-esteem and the loss of appetite and sexual drive. He finds it difficult to perform on his job. The symptoms tend toward lows in the morning and improvement toward evening, not unlike the progress of an alcohol hangover. Depressive episodes may last for months and then clear up spontaneously. Some recur regularly. Sadness isn't always a feature in cases of depression. But agitated behavior, strong feelings of worthlessness and pessimism about the future nearly always characterize the disease.

What should you do if you suspect you might be subject to the malady? First, you should try a little self-analysis to determine whether those moods you have are normal aspects of the human condition or abnormal. Check yourself against the following simple list of statements about yourself concerning emotional outlook, motivation, self-image, physical symptoms and behavior.

Dr. Aaron Beck of the Depression Research Unit at Philadelphia

General Hospital and others* worked up this "depression inventory." Select those statements which you believe apply best to you. Then add the numbers assigned to each statement that you picked.

A (Mood)
    0   I do not feel sad
    1   I feel blue or sad
    2a I am blue or sad all the time
        and I can't snap out of it
    2b I am so sad or unhappy that it
        is very painful
    3   I am so sad or unhappy that I
        can't stand it

B (Pessimism)
    0   I am not particularly pessimistic
        or discouraged about the future
    1a I feel discouraged about the future
    2a I feel I have nothing to look forward to
    2b I feel that I won't ever get over
        my troubles
    3   I feel that the future is hopeless
        and that things cannot improve

C (Sense of Failure)
    0   I do not feel like a failure
    1   I feel I have failed more than the
        average person
    2a I feel I have accomplished very
        little that is worthwhile or that
        means anything
    2b As I look back on my life all I can
        see is a lot of failures
    3   I feel I am a complete failure as
        a person (parent, husband, wife)

*Drs. A.T. Beck, C.H. Ward, M. Mendelson, J. Mock and J. Erbaugh, "An Inventory for Measuring Depression," *Archives of General Psychiatry,* Vol. 4, pp. 561–571, June 1961, an American Medical Association publication.

D (Lack of Satisfaction)
   0   I am not particularly dissatisfied
   1a I feel bored most of the time
   1b I don't enjoy things the way I
       used to
   2   I don't get satisfaction out of
       anything any more
   3   I am dissatisfied with everything

E (Guilty Feeling)
   0   I don't feel particularly guilty
   1   I feel bad or unworthy a good
       part of the time
   2a I feel quite guilty
   2b I feel bad or unworthy practically
       all the time now
   3   I feel as though I am very bad or worthless

F (Sense of Punishment)
   0   I don't feel I am being punished
   1   I have a feeling that something bad may happen to me
   2   I feel I am being punished or will be punished
   3a I feel I deserve to be punished
   3b I want to be punished

G (Self-Hate)
   0   I don't feel disappointed in myself
   1a I am disappointed in myself
   1b I don't like myself
   2   I am disgusted with myself
   3   I hate myself

H (Self-Accusations)
   0   I don't feel I am any worse than anybody else
   1   I am very critical of myself for my weaknesses or mistakes
   2a I blame myself for everything that goes wrong

I (Self-punitive Wishes)
   0   I don't have any thoughts of harming myself
   1   I have thoughts of harming myself but I would not carry them out
   2a I feel I would be better off dead
   2b I have definite plans about committing suicide

2c I feel my family would be better off if I were dead
3 I would kill myself if I could

J (Crying Spells)
  0 I don't cry any more than usual
  1 I cry more now than I used to
  2 I cry all the time now. I can't stop it
  3 I used to be able to cry but now I can't cry at all even though I want to

K (Irritability)
  0 I am no more irritated now than I ever am
  1 I get annoyed or irritated more easily than I used to
  2 I feel irritated all the time
  3 I don't get irritated at all at the things that used to irritate me

L (Social Withdrawal)
  0 I have not lost interest in other people
  1 I am less interested in other people than I used to be
  2 I have lost most of my interest in other people and have little feeling for them
  3 I have lost all my interest in other people and don't care about them at all

M (Indecisiveness)
  0 I make decisions about as well as ever
  1 I am less sure of myself now and try to put off making decisions
  2 I can't make decisions anymore without help
  3 I can't make any decisions at all anymore

N (Body Image)
  0 I don't feel I look any worse than I used to
  1 I am worried that I am looking old or unattractive
  2 I feel that there are permanent changes in my appearance and they make me look unattractive
  3 I feel that I am ugly or repulsive looking

O (Work Inhibition)
  0 I can work about as well as before
  1a It takes extra effort to get started at doing something
  2 I have to push myself very hard to do anything
  3 I can't do any work at all

P (Sleep Disturbance)
  0 I can sleep as well as usual
  1 I wake up more tired in the morning than I used to
  2 I wake up 1–2 hours earlier than usual and find it hard to get back
     to sleep
  3 I wake up early every day and can't get more than 5 hours' sleep

Q (Fatigability)
  0 I don't get any more tired than usual
  1 I get tired more easily than I used to
  2 I get tired from doing anything
  3 I get too tired to do anything

R (Loss of Appetite)
  0 My appetite is no worse than usual
  1 My appetite is not as good as it used to be
  2 My appetite is much worse now
  3 I have no appetite at all any more

S (Weight Loss)
  0 I haven't lost much weight, if any, lately
  1 I have lost more than 5 pounds
  2 I have lost more than 10 pounds
  3 I have lost more than 15 pounds

T (Somatic Preoccupation)
  0 I am no more concerned about my health than usual
  1 I am concerned about aches and pains or upset stomach or
     constipation or other unpleasant feelings in my body
  2 I am so concerned with how I feel or what I feel that it's hard to
     think of much else
  3 I am completely absorbed in what I feel

U (Loss of Libido)
  0 I have not noticed any recent change in my interest in sex
  1 I am less interested in sex than I used to be
  2 I am much less interested in sex now
  3 I have lost interest in sex completely

A total score of less than 4 indicates normality. A score of 4 to 7 suggests a mild depression, 8 to 15 moderate, and 16 or higher, severe.

If you score eight or higher, consider seeing your physician or psychiatrist.

In his own research, Dr. Beck has identified several personality prototypes predisposed to depression. One is the individual who lost a parent or was otherwise deprived during childhood. On the other hand, some over-achievers in childhood and early adult life, when they received much love and attention, later learn they can't succeed in everything. "They haven't learned the taste of defeat," says the Philadelphia psychiatrist, "and they can't cope with it."

While there is no magic formula to relieve depression, psychotherapeutic techniques, drugs, and electroshock therapy have brought dramatic relief. Despite the fact that we may now be suffering an epidemic of depression, especially among the young, the outlook for today's victims is brighter than it has ever been. "After all," asks Dr. Bertram S. Brown, director of the National Institute of Mental Health, "how many other diseases are there where, with accurate diagnosis and really effective care, you've got a 95 per cent chance of getting back to totally full functioning?"

After fifteen years of agonizing, Ted finally accepted the fact that he suffered from a fairly common disease and not some socially reprehensible malady. He put himself into the hands of a psychiatrist. Within a year, he had recovered sufficiently to accept a job offer with another firm where he at last could try the administrative side of the business. As his psychiatrist pointed out: "What have you to lose? If this doesn't work out, you can always return to straight selling. But you have to answer this question about yourself that has nagged you so long: Can I make it as a manager? If you learn you can, great. If you find you cannot, you can at least put your mind to rest on that score and know that you can still be a damn good salesman. You first have to find out what you are. When you learn that, then you can accept your limitations."

Yet what about people who are normal, but still suffer from doubt and irresolution that afflict all of us occasionally? Many of the other fables touch on this condition, notably "Belling the Cat" and "The Man That Pleased None."

Modern Precept for Promotion: "If your job-related fears seem abnormal, you can get help in controlling them."

"Brag is not belief."

The Frog and the Bull

"I'm as big as that Bull," cried the Frog
As he huffed and he puffed on his log.
The nearby Bull looked bored,
Then in derision roared.
And the Frog fell back into the bog.

Aesop's Moral: "Brag is not belief."

The Contemporary Illustration

Melvin N. carefully slid from under the covers of his twin bed, shuffled into his slippers and slipped into his bathrobe. He sighed with relief that he had succeeded in getting out of the bedroom without awakening his wife. He couldn't face her, not after last night.

He had come home Friday evening full of his grievances. Instead of gradually dissipating as they usually did while he recounted them to Emily over cocktails, they worsened in his mind.

"I've been selling for thirty years," he railed. "I won't have a pip-squeak of a sales manager tell me I blew the Acme order. I was selling when that kid wasn't yet out of his crib. I told him from the beginning that we might lose Acme."

Emily stirred her drink with her finger, as though she might find a fish in it. "I thought the Acme thing was a cinch."

"Cinch? Far from it — a bitch from day one."

"Yet you told me it was a cinch." She licked her finger reflectively. "Just a week or so ago. Right here."

Mel had waved the interruption aside. "If those words came out, it was the drink talking, not me. I've been selling long enough to know a bitch when I see one. I was willing to take it on because I've pulled some coups in my day."

"Name one."

"Christ, Emily, don't give me a hard time. I've already had a tough day. And you know what else that bastard said?"

"You mean the sales manager?"

Mel slapped his hands on his knees. "Who the hell do you think I mean, the president of the United States?"

"You deal with so many bastards, I didn't know which one."

Mel eyed her narrowly before continuing, "The sales manager criticized the way I dress. The length of my hair. The nerve of the guy!"

Emily looked reflective. "That does seem like going too far. But you do need another dye job on your hair. The gray's showing again. And men's hair styles are getting a little shorter, I notice. As to your clothes, I like the young look. You know that." Then she added sweetly, "But you don't have to sell to me, or do you?"

The real argument had started then, one of their worst. Mel picked up the morning paper from the front steps and stepped back in to sit and read it. He couldn't concentrate on it, so upset was he about last night and the earlier events at the office. Emily had called him a braggart.

"You're your own worst enemy," she had said. "You make claims you can't meet. No wonder the sales manager was mad. Knowing you, I bet you told him the Acme order was a cinch. Then when you didn't get it, of course he was disappointed and took out his disappointment on you. Why do you make trouble for yourself like this?"

Why indeed? Most people who boast do it to reassure themselves, primarily. Related reasons are to impress others and to gain advancement. Emily had bluntly told Mel that he boasted more now than when he was younger.

While boasting doesn't correlate particularly with age, it does track with a person's sense of inadequacy. For example, the greater his sense of career frustration, the more prone he is to the psychological relief of boasting. A person in his fifties who suspects he'll never become president of the company or even a manager may succumb to braggadocio.

If an adult, the braggart seldom shows his colors with crude boasts. Indeed, he's often surprisingly creative and finds inventive ways to brag. Examples:

- He makes frequent references to former accomplishments, some of them years in the past, and uses ingenious excuses to mention them.
- He makes light of all potential difficulties, despite having trouble with some assignments.
- He's defensive about shortcomings and mistakes or even refuses to acknowledge them.
- His dress and mannerisms often relate to another age group, either older or younger.
- He dislikes all authority, but especially the current boss; he criticizes all authority but to others, not to the authority itself.

Sometimes braggadocio works, especially with people who don't know you well. Furthermore, everyone boasts in an inoffensive way from time to time. I'm not dealing with that here. I'm dealing with the persistent variety that interferes with a person's career because it inevitably irritates others. And, more importantly, because it hides from the braggart his own faults and thus inhibits or totally prevents a remedy. Boasts eventually sound credible only to the boaster.

Mel had reached the point where even his wife no longer believed him. As he sat in his armchair, at last he admitted that truth. But what could he do?

The person who brags too much shares some of the same problems with one who drinks excessively. He has come to depend psychologically on the boasts or the drink. His first hurdle is to admit he has a problem; his second, to stop it. Only the rare alcoholic can cure himself by cutting down on his drinking; most must stop altogether. The same holds for the braggart. He must stop entirely making empty claims.

This doesn't mean you can't sell yourself. But you must learn to do it differently. Let your actions and the results of your actions do your selling. Teachers of writing skills say, "Don't tell, show." The same holds in selling yourself.

The braggart shares another hazard with the alcoholic in overcoming the habit — backsliding. They both must guard against it, or perish. Braggarts and alcoholics also are often imaginative people. They can rationalize with ease and invent excuses to boast or drink at the first sign of stress.

Mel was thinking along these lines as Emily emerged from the bedroom.

"You're right," he said.

"About what?"

"The boasting. I've got to stop it."

"I'll help, do whatever I can, Mel. Just ask me."

On Monday, Mel entered the sales manager's office.

"I've been thinking it over," he confessed, "and I did botch the Acme order. I'm going to do my damnedest to see that it doesn't happen again."

Nor did it happen again. Although Mel did backslide a few times, he caught himself before he did himself serious damage. His sales performance improved, and so did his relations with his boss. He even had his hair cut a little shorter and made subtle modifications in his style of dress. He felt he had solved his problem when he overheard his sales manager telling the company president, "I'm going to put Mel on this one. He turned us around on the Acme matter, and I'll bet he could do the same here."

Modern Precept for Promotion: "Your performance itself will advance you faster than your talk about it."

"Beware of enterprises where the risks
aren't equal."

The Geese and the Cranes

Geese and Cranes gorged in fields of grain
Until the strong farmer raised Cain.
The light-winged Cranes fled
But the Geese, over fed,
Were unable to fly — to their pain.

Aesop's Moral: "Beware of enterprises where the risks aren't equal."

The Contemporary Illustration

Louis M., an ambitious young account executive with a midwestern advertising firm, took a job at a large salary increase with a Texas company that marketed a line of inexpensive costume jewelry throughout the United States.

Within less than a year, Lou lost that job and returned to the Midwest where he was happy to find work with a steel company's ad department. His Texas adventure had proved a bad risk on two counts. First, he went into a kind of retail business about which he knew almost nothing. In his agency days, he had serviced accounts in manufacturing. While some of them retailed their products, none had given him the experience to deal confidently with the advertising and marketing problems of costume jewelry.

While his inexperience created risk number one, he might have survived that if he hadn't overlooked risk number two. His wife and family didn't enjoy Houston with its heat and humidity. Lou had partly taken into account the first risk, although he had underestimated its nature. He thought he would merely have to learn some new advertising and publicity techniques for costume jewelry; he had not reckoned on the need to reorient his whole advertising philosophy. Formerly, he had concentrated on good-looking ads and a gentlemanly approach to publicity. In jewelry, he never did learn that the appearance of the ad was secondary to whether it sold and that gentlemanly public relations was a concept foreign to the business.

But he had completely overlooked the possibility that the second risk would even surface. Didn't everybody love Texas? Everybody did but his family. Thus, the imperfectly perceived professional challenges and the unlooked-for domestic hazards both combined to overwhelm him.

Gary I., on the other hand, took a different approach to the risks involved in an opportunity that opened for him. As a specialist on employee benefits for a large manufacturer, he had an assured future and a good income. An insurance brokerage firm offered him the possibility of a much larger (or smaller) income and a not-so-assured future as a salesman. On the face of it, Gary would seem to be a fool even to consider such an exchange. Yet he did — so seriously that he accepted it. Here's how Gary saw the chances:

1. The new job offered the possibility of more money. But if he didn't do well as a salesman of employee benefit plans to business and industry, he could always return as a specialist on such plans for a large company.

2. The new job promised to provide more varied and interesting work than the position he now held. At thirty-eight years of age, he already was a little bored with his present work.

3. The insurance broker had its headquarters in the same city as his present employer, so he would not have to uproot his family.

4. The new job would require more travel than his present one, but he liked that. Part of his current boredom stemmed from the fact that he seldom got out of his office.

5. He would be away more from his family. Nevertheless, his wife wanted him to take the offer because she had sensed his growing restlessness as a benefits specialist.

So Gary took the selling job and his appraisal of the risks proved approximately right. He didn't make quite as much money as he had hoped (you seldom do), but within a year he was earning 40 per cent more than formerly. The new work was even more interesting than he had hoped. While the travel load was a little heavier than he expected (it often is), he didn't mind it and his family didn't complain.

But what do you do when your appraisal indicates the risks aren't worth taking? You refuse the alleged promotion because it won't result in a true advancement.

Yet, the great trouble with standpat decisions is that you will never know for sure if your judgment was right. You may see how another person will fare who did accept the offer. If he fails, you can congratulate yourself; if he succeeds, you can eat your heart out — but not really because that person is not you. In short, you will never know.

That dislike of never knowing acts as a fatal lure sometimes. It contributed to Lou's ill-fated Texas decision. He had turned down the offer once. Then he had changed his mind because he couldn't bear not knowing how events would turn out. You may wonder, too. While it's human to do so, it's also a waste of time. Try to avoid the what-might-have-been state of mind.

Yet, poor analysis of the risks lies at the bottom of most flawed decisions. Note that I say "analysis of the risks." If you are ambitious, you of course must take some risks. When you fear the risk itself, you're in trouble. Professor Silvan Tomkins of Princeton University believes that success "without willingness to gamble is highly improbable." Many people are embarrassed by failures; truly ambitious people are almost proud of them.

Lou eventually became vice president of advertising and public relations for the steel company he joined after his Texas adventure. By that time, he could mention it without pain as "my Texas taxes," meaning the cost of the episode to him financially. It had taught him the value of analysis, and in the long run that repaid him many times for the expense of Texas.

Dr. John M. Schlien of the University of Chicago, feels that the ambitious person must also "be willing to make mistakes despite the probable effect on others." Lou and Gary both were willing to do that.

The fear of risks also ties in with the fears of failure, criticism, and the loss of self-esteem. The causes stem from other factors as well. For instance, our educational system stresses caution from kindergarten on. Of course, children often remain rash and foolhardy, but the net effect of the constant harping is to breed caution into many people by the time they are adults — an unexpected side effect that remains a habit of mind with them for the rest of their lives.

The industrial environment tends to accentuate fear of risks, too. Safety is preached constantly. The doctrine of "the prudent man" with his "feet on the ground" lies implicit in much management training. I don't oppose safety and prudence, but I do urge that you don't give these qualities overwhelming weight when you consider your strategy for advancement.

Another aspect of risk concerns the kinds of chances you choose to take — defensive or offensive. Or, stated another way, you can decide to maximize your gains. When Gary moved to the brokerage firm, he took an offensive risk; he hoped to maximize his gains, a wish that was realized. When Lou returned to the Midwest from Texas, he was taking another kind of risk — a defensive one this time because he wanted to minimize his losses, a hope that also was eventually realized.

In analyzing the risk, understand its defensive or offensive nature because that can make a big difference. For example, Lou took a far less dangerous risk in his defensive move than in his offensive shift.

The defensive chance usually is less hazardous than the offensive because the need to stop losses is often powerful and outweighs every negative aspect.

Sometimes people make a move only to learn they face a risk that they didn't know existed or that develops after they have made the shift. In the fable of the "Dog in the Manger," Sally T. had almost no way of knowing in advance that Belle Y. would have such a baleful influence on her teaching career. The best course, then, is to leave, taking a defensive chance aimed at minimizing losses.

You can argue that Sally could have dealt with the risk positively — by handling Belle more skillfully. Yet, this was Sally's first real job. She was too inexperienced to know how to defuse Belle.

A risk almost impossible to defend against is that which develops soon after the supposed advancement. Gary became a victim of such a situation. Eighteen months after joining the brokerage firm, his boss died. The chemistry didn't mix well between Gary and the new man. Gary eventually left — not for a benefits specialist job with a big employer but for another brokerage firm.

Note that in the cases of both Sally and Gary people proved to be the major element of risk. So, when you appraise your move, study your new associates as closely as possible. They constitute the most serious hazard.

Modern Precept for Promotion: "Accept only sensible risks when you make your move."

"Don't throw away the future for
immediate but illusory gains."

The Goose with the Golden Eggs

A greedy rich man's goose renown'd
Laid golden eggs by the pound.
But he killed the poor thing,
Quicker fortune to bring,
And got only flesh by the mound.

Aesop's Moral: "Don't throw away the future for immediate but illusory gains."

The Contemporary Illustration

Quentin N. gave up his job selling mutual funds for a New York firm to take over his father's business as a manufacturers' representative selling specialty steel products in Connecticut and Massachusetts.

His father had long urged such a move, but Quentin had resisted, both because the business couldn't support two men and because he and his father didn't always get along well. Both were strong willed men who liked to have their own way. Yet when the father promised to retire completely, Quentin at last agreed to take over his sales business.

An early danger signal started flying when Quentin's parents decided after a three months' trial that Florida didn't suit them as a place for retirement. They returned to Hartford where Quentin and his wife had moved, having purchased the parents' home. While the older couple went into an apartment, they made it clear they didn't approve of structural changes in the house which Quentin had remodelled to permit him an office in his home.

"It's much better to have your office downtown in the business area," grumbled his father. "You can meet people for lunch easier."

"But I'm on the road three-fourths of the time, not in downtown Hartford," countered Quentin. "An office in the house maximizes my time with the family. And it saves money because Beth can act as a secretary when I'm out."

At first the father said nothing about the decline in business under Quentin's aegis, even though it meant less income than he had expected from the modest override Quentin gave him as payment for the going sales organization. When no substantial improvement had occurred after a year, the father complained.

"Dad, you know steel sales generally are down. We've got to grin and bear it."

But Dad could do neither and began making "suggestions." Soon father and son drifted into near warfare. An irrelevant event triggered the final break. Quentin's mother criticized Beth's taste in redecorating the house. Quentin and family returned to New York and selling mutual funds. The father left retirement with relief to take up his business again.

In an attempt to pave the way to the future, Quentin's Hartford sojourn had proved a wasteful detour. In resuming his mutual funds sales, he had lost many customers in the fifteen months he had been away from that business and had to start over almost from the beginning.

Events finally proved to Quentin that he had made the wrong short-term moves. Unwittingly, he had sacrificed the goose, laying modest golden eggs, for a mound of flesh.

Does it ever make sense to "kill the goose?" Yes, in unusual cases. Frank L. (in the fable of the "Dog in the Manger") wisely promoted his star lawyer, Ray, to a divisional position where he could no longer directly assist his former boss. But Frank knew that the talented Ray would have left shortly on his own hook. In the end, a fortunate turnabout took place because the high-flying Ray promoted Frank to a better position in another company.

Helen O. faced a more difficult dilemma. At fifty-three, she was the respected senior buyer for women's clothing in a department store of a middle-sized Pennsylvania city. She could retire at reduced pension as early as age sixty and at full retirement benefits at sixty-five — provided she still worked for the store at the time of retirement.

Yet Helen needed money. As a widow herself, she well knew the difficulties facing her daughter and infant grandson who had just lost husband and father in an automobile accident. Both had also been injured in the same tragedy, and insurance failed to cover all of the expenses.

A women's dress manufacturer had long been attempting to hire Helen as a sales representative with the prospect of earning 50 per cent more than the store paid, but she had resisted the offer because of the store's pension fund to which she had contributed for more than twenty years. If she left, all she would get from it would be what she had contributed plus interest.

Helen left for the dress firm, sacrificing her pension and an assured future with the store. She used the money returned to her from the pension fund to clear up medical bills stemming from the accident. Her added income helped support her daughter and grandson until the daughter could redirect her life.

Not so incidentally, the daughter eventually joined the store as an assistant buyer in women's wear. And Helen found she enjoyed her new selling job. So, under special circumstances, it may pay to kill the goose. You may acquire another.

Sometimes you must resist the well-meaning but unwise advice of friends to kill the goose that lays the golden eggs. Ernie L. faced that problem. In a corporate reorganization, he found himself demoted, although his salary wasn't cut. Indignant friends urged him to quit. He did survey the job market and soon discovered the slim pickings for a forty-nine-year-old marine engineering manager.

Ernie stuck it out as a plain marine engineer and showed no signs of wounded pride or other hurt feelings. The right offer from another company would have intrigued and perhaps won him, but none materialized because of the state of the marine engineering business.

He did not register with any recruiting firm. "I avoided that action for two reasons," he said. "First, it's much better for a prospective employer to come to you than vice versa. Your bargaining position is much improved. Second, the word often gets around that a recruiter is active on your behalf. This rarely happens because the recruiter talks out of turn. It occurs because the people he approaches let the tidbit drop after the second drink at a business lunch. I didn't want this to happen because I wanted things kept smooth and clean with this outfit so that I could climb back as a manager when business picked up."

Ernie was a wise man. Business did pick up and he again became a manager. Two years later, he won another promotion, this time to manage a bigger and more stable component in the company.

Similarly, Jack M. (in the "Fox and the Grapes") wisely refused one offer of promotion and waited until one came along a year later that suited him better.

The cases of Ernie and Jack indicate that sometimes seemingly foolish, short-term moves are wise in the long run.

The other side of this coin involves the seemingly safe long-term career move that backfires. Wilma W. had six years to go before she became due for a pension granted to eligible teachers in her state. The junior high school where she had taught for more than thirty years had changed drastically because the community it served had become almost completely black in population. As English instructor and white, Wilma found herself more and more estranged from her students. They scorned Hawthorne's *A Scarlet Letter* and were bored when she changed that reading assignment for Betty Smith's *A Tree Grows in Brooklyn*. She became physically ill as a result of an episode that began when someone wrote "W.W. stands for white witch" on her chalkboard.

As things grew more and more uncomfortable for her, she applied for a transfer to the other junior high school in the system, but no openings were available. Furthermore, the same metamorphosis threatened that institution that had already befallen her own. She considered applying for other teaching positions in her state whereby she would remain in the same pension system, but nothing came as a result of two applications she submitted. Furthermore, she didn't relish moving from her apartment where she had lived for a quarter century.

So, Wilma tried to weather out the last six years. She made it for two years until her heart attack. She survived that and gratefully took a disability pension. However, at fifty-seven she had become a semi-invalid, her useful life over.

Wilma's "safe" decision probably ruined her health. She herself regretted not leaving a situation with which she could not cope. She should have sacrificed her pension and saved her health. As it was, her disability benefits were only about half of what a full pension would have been.

Earl A., whom we last encountered hoarding employees unnecessarily in the fable of the "Dog in the Manger," made a different kind of "safe" long-term move that ruined his career — at least with the employer that fired him after catching him playing such tricks. Earl slid into the same tactical maneuvers with his next employer. Some people never learn.

From the cases of Wilma and Earl we see that we should watch out for the "safe" long-term move. We have also observed the danger of wrong short-term actions, although seemingly foolish short-term moves may turn out to be wise in the long run or at least justified by special circumstances. In short, in your career planning, weigh the short-term and the long-term for a balanced strategy.

Modern Precept for Promotion: "The right job action for the present means the right career for the future."

"Save for a rainy day."

The Grasshopper and the Ant

Grasshopper came on a rainy day
To beg food from the Ant, come what may.
"Save when it's dry," cried Ant.
Grasshopper said, "I can't
Because then is the time when I play."

Aesop's Moral: "Save for a rainy day."

The Contemporary Illustration

Guy D. stared at the note on his desk. "Please see Martin," it read. It was unusual on two counts. First, it was written by his boss, Jack Martin, himself, and not by the office secretary, giving a phone message. Secondly, Martin usually called. He wasn't the note-writing type. Guy buzzed the secretary. "Has Martin been trying to reach me?" he asked when she came to his office.

"Yes, for two days."

Guy slammed his hands down on the desk. "Why didn't you ring me at the apartment?"

"Mr. Martin said I wasn't to do that."

"For God's sake, Phoebe, you haven't let that stop you before. You could've called me anyhow."

"Maybe I'm getting tired of covering up for you."

Guy got up and went to her, to put his arm around her, but she evaded him. "Now come on, Pheeb, honey, don't be like that."

"Don't call me Pheeb. And I'm not your honey." Guy laughed. "Oh, it's like that, is it, Miss Atwood?"

"Yes, it is — and from now on. You're never going to stand me up again."

"Phoebe, you promised you wouldn't hold that against me. I explained. I had too much to drink. I plain forgot our date. In fact, I forgot everything. I passed out. I'm not proud of it, but can't you forgive me? I swear it'll never happen again."

Phoebe shrugged shapely shoulders. "You've told me a dozen times, 'It'll never happen again.' Now I believe you because I'm never going out with you again." She slid past him and added, "You better see Martin on the double. And you better have a grade A story for him."

Guy grimaced and glanced at his watch to learn with dismay that it was already nearly eleven. He strolled down to the end of the corridor, to the panelled door on which was lettered, John R. Martin, vice president-sales. He went in and smiled at the middle-aged woman at the desk. "What a pretty dress, Grace. New, isn't it?"

"I've worn it at least once a week for about a year," she said. "Mr. Martin will see you at two this afternoon."

"But I've got a sales call scheduled for two."

"Mr. Martin said to cancel whatever you had and be here at two. He can't see you now. He's in a meeting."

"Oh, well, I'll go on in. Would've been here earlier if I'd known. Meeting on Friday? That's unusual."

Grace got up and blocked his way. "This isn't a regular sales meeting, and it's not for you, Guy. Come back at two."

Guy carefully rationed his drinks at lunch, taking only two Scotches. He had tried to pick up a luncheon companion from among the other salesmen at the office, but none had been available. He invited Phoebe; he was not surprised when she refused. He had tried to pump her about the meeting and the other ominous signals. She claimed to know nothing.

He presented himself at Martin's office promptly at two, and was called in immediately.

Martin neither smiled nor rose when he entered. "Did you cancel your two o'clock appointment alright?"

For a moment Guy looked puzzled. He had forgotten the spur-of-the-moment lie he had given Grace earlier. "Yes, yes. No trouble."

Martin looked at some notes he had on his desk. "Your sales performance is way off, Guy. Down 30 per cent this quarter from a year earlier."

Guy waved his hands. "I know. I'm sick about it. But business is off generally. Next. . ."

Martin interrupted. "Business isn't off generally. As a whole we're up this quarter — despite your poor showing."

"I can't understand that, Jack. I've been running into nothing but gloom and doom from the purchasing agents."

"How many of these purchasing agents have you been seeing?"

Guy waved his hand. "The usual number. You've got my sales sheets."

Martin opened a drawer and pulled out a sheaf of papers that Guy with a sinking feeling recognized as his reports.

Martin flipped through them. "Here's one from Western Industries that indicates you called on them ten days ago. Fowler there says you weren't in to see him, just called him on the phone. He tells me you haven't been in to see him in person for three months. He's pissed off, and I don't blame him. Threatened to take his business elsewhere. Fortunately, he's reconsidered. Higgins has the account now, as of yesterday." Martin paused; when Guy said nothing, he continued. "I wonder how many other accounts you've been servicing like Western."

"Jack, I admit I goofed badly with Western, but I've been not feeling too hot lately. I cut corners with Western. I should not have."

Martin riffled through other reports. "You've been cutting corners with others, too — Atlantic, Hudson Industries and Enterprise Machine. After Western's complaints, I began checking your other accounts. I've only had time to do those three because each has given me an earful. In fact, yesterday Higgins and I had to make a trip to Enterprise. You have been making personal calls there, it seems, but on the purchasing agent's secretary, not on the PA himself."

"Good God, Jack, what is this, the Inquisition? Sure, I've had a few drinks with the girl there. The only way to sell her boss is to have an 'in' with his secretary."

Martin put the reports back in his desk. "That kind of selling went out with Willie Loman in *Death of a Salesman*. For your information, that girl at Enterprise happens to be the president's niece. All your little tidbits of gossip got right back to him. You had no business telling her about the credit problems we're having with other customers."

Guy slid forward in his chair. "Come on, Jack, I told her practically nothing that she didn't already know or strongly suspect."

"You told her plenty," Martin said flatly. "The president gave it all back to Higgins and me yesterday. That's bad enough, but now Enterprise is wondering what you're telling their competitors about them." The sales vice president paused. "Enterprise wants nothing more to do with you. Higgins has your account from now on."

Guy leaped to his feet. "Damm it, Martin. What are you doing to me? You've taken away two of my best accounts."

"I'm firing you, Guy. Get your stuff out of your desk and be out of this building by five o'clock."

"Christ! What kind of notice is that?"

Martin pulled an envelope from his pocket. "Here's a check for two weeks' salary in lieu of notice."

"Two weeks' salary! That's peanuts and you know it. I make twice as much as that on commissions."

Guy disdainfully tore the envelope without opening it. The action seemed to quiet him because he sat down and stared at the pieces in his hand.

"Look, Jack, you can't be serious about this. I've goofed, I admit. But I can sell, you know that. For three years now I've proved it."

Martin sighed. "Yes, you can sell — when you feel like it. That's why I've put up with you for three years. The trouble is, you seem to be feeling less like selling with every passing month. You're volume has been sliding for the past seven months. Higgins and I looked at your records only this morning."

"Higgins!" Guy twisted in his chair in disgust. "That bastard's been angling for my accounts ever since he came here."

"He hasn't, Guy. But if he had, all he had to do was wait you out. You've been asking for it — faking sales reports, cooking your expense accounts, working only two or three days a week, chasing every presentable and half-presentable female that came your way."

"Come on, Jack. It's not as bad as that. I've been sick lately."

"Hungover, to be exact."

Guy looked up. "Alright, that too. Jack, this is a helluva shock."

Martin fiddled with a paperweight on his desk. "Why should it be such a surprise? Consolidated let you go for many of the same reasons before you came here. Remember our little talks when you first joined me? I said I would can you in a minute if you repeated the Consolidated shenanigans with me. Well I didn't fire you in a minute, although I should have. I looked the other way when that business with Phoebe Atwood started. I said nothing about all those Monday sick days you had. But I've warned you several times about your expense accounts, and I've told you before about phony sales reports."

Guy stared at the pieces of torn check and envelope still in his hands. "Give me another chance, Jack. I swear I'll straighten out."

Martin stood up, looking at the torn check. "Have you got anything in the bank?"

Guy shook his head. "Less than a hundred."

The vice president sighed. "I'll have Grace make out a new check for you — two weeks' salary plus two weeks of average commissions. Good-bye, Guy."

Modern Precept for Promotion: "Assets frittered away are gone forever."

"Slow and steady sometimes wins the race."

The Hare and the Tortoise

It was a silly race to call
Between Hare and Tortoise — that's all.
But the Hare took a nap
While Tortoise took a lap
To win the whole thing in a crawl.

Aesop's Moral: "Slow and steady sometimes wins the race."

The Contemporary Illustration

Jim R. is in prison now; a flamboyant career guiding a high-flying conglomerate brought to an abrupt halt with his conviction for stock fraud. The accountants, lawyers and others who might have advised the thirty-two-year-old Jim about the illegality of his schemes either didn't have access to him or, in some cases, didn't speak up. Most were also young, dazzled by the conglomerate's success and all too eager to believe whatever portraits of unlimited profit Jim painted.

In court, he testified that he didn't know that he was committing any crimes. Of course that didn't hold any water with the judge, because ignorance of the law is no excuse. But non-lawyers didn't believe him either. Yet Jim really hadn't realized he had violated any laws. In his headlong drive for riches, he never stopped to ask.

Albert J., forty-five, who had been a vice president of one of the score of companies that Jim had acquired, is now trying to reassemble the more profitable pieces of Jim's ramshackle structure. After a careful study of Albert's reorganization proposal, the banks have extended him a line of credit that he believes will help him to rebuild the conglomerate. Although Albert plans this on far more modest lines than Jim's visionary dreams, lawyers, accountants and bankers will monitor his every move to keep him on the track of legality and success.

Albert was the oldest executive working in the firms acquired who had remained. He had stubbornly refused to leave his company to which he had already devoted twenty-three years of his life, even though he had disapproved when the family which had owned it sold out to Jim and even though he had increasingly opposed the conglomerate's approach to business generally. During the three years of Jim's ownership, he had fought a holding action resisting short-sighted moves for quick and high profits. At the crash, Albert's division was the only one in the entire setup still showing respectable earnings.

Albert is on his way to winning a race in which he had contested unwillingly. Other people compete for success willingly. Floyd F. entered in the eager category. An electrical equipment manufacturer recruited him and Larry S. in the same year for a marketing training program. Floyd so clearly outshone Larry at the start that Larry seemed dull by comparison. When Floyd quit to join a competitor just as he had completed the training, the manufacturer became even more annoyed than usual if such departures occur, because he felt he had lost a sure winner.

Larry stayed on, a good but not brilliant marketing man. For several years, Floyd apparently fulfilled his promise — but unfortunately with the rival. When he left that manufacturer for a promotion with still another, the original employer lost track of him. Almost a decade had passed when Floyd turned up again, applying for a job with the first company.

By this time, ironically, Larry had become assistant marketing manager, responsible, among other things, for recruiting sales personnel. He investigated Floyd's references, as he would any applicant's. While the company did not blackball former employees, a somewhat unusual omission signalled caution to Larry. For the past year, Floyd said he had been in business for himself as a manufacturers' representative. However, he did not list any of the manufacturers he represented.

"Cats and dogs," Floyd explained airily. "I couldn't get any reputable outfits because the good ones sell direct. That's why I had to drop out of the rep business."

But Larry knew this wasn't strictly true. Smaller well-known competitors did sell through representatives. Suspicious now, Larry probed more deeply than usual with the references given and eventually learned the real story. Floyd had become an alcoholic. As a manufacturers' rep, he couldn't hold a reputable account. The people listed as references reluctantly admitted the difficulty when Larry asked about it directly. Floyd did not get rehired.

Alcoholism has resulted in more lost races in business, industry, education and government than any other malady. Between 4 and 8 per cent of the nation's work force are alcoholics, costing business $8 billion to $10 billion a year in absenteeism, botched work and related costs. Nobody knows precisely why someone becomes an alcoholic, but a common characteristic of the victims is that they often showed potential for success at one point in their careers. Either they began drinking excessively because they couldn't achieve their potential or because they couldn't cope with the psychological tensions that success sometimes brings.

Some races for promotion occur even when at least one participant doesn't or won't recognize that he's in a contest.

Harvey B. was an assistant buyer in furniture for a chain of department stores in a metropolitan area. Connie S. held a similar post in the enterprise. While many women were the chief buyers in dresses, toys and other areas where females naturally were the principal customers, no lady had ever been chief buyer in furniture. Harvey considered her eccentric, scarcely worthy of consideration as a rival, making allusions to her among his friends as "my Ms. Women's Lib."

But he softened the onus of the heavy humor with indulgence. "When she first came here," he would recount, "I had to tell her what an escritoire was. I think she thought it was French for some sexy bedroom piece."

Over several years as an assistant furniture buyer, Connie learned far more about her field than the French name for writing desk. She was largely responsible for the introduction of a modified warehouse selling technique to compete with the discount houses. She sharpened an uncanny intuition in judging coming style trends. She developed a strong department in bedroom furniture for teenagers, which formerly had been virtually nonexistent.

When she was named chief furniture buyer, the promotion surprised no one — except Harvey. "She belongs in lingerie, not furniture," he protested. "And I've been teaching her the trade for years." He had taught her, as had every salesperson and customer for years. She had made herself a professional while Harvey had remained a dilettante.

Ann V. and Carol T. joined New York City's school system as elementary school teachers at the same time. After the first year, Carol left for a post in a private school.

"I can't stand the bureaucracy in the public system," she would explain. "I spent more time filling out their forms than I did in grading papers. And the children! No manners. No discipline. Finally, I couldn't stand being just a number in that setup. Imagine — 70,000 teachers in New York Public Schools!"

Ann stayed on in the nation's largest school organization. She filled out the forms and had enough persistence to get them reduced in number and simplified. She became an effective disciplinarian and gave some children their first lessons in deportment. And she coped with the problems of size, carving a niche for herself in her elementary school to the extent that she eventually became its principal.

And Carol? She has taught in several private schools. She left teaching briefly to travel selling elementary textbooks for a publisher, but she didn't like that and returned to a church-related school.

"I refuse to be the 'Miss Chips' at the County Day school," she explains. "I'm going to try this Lutheran setup, but I'm not going to stay if the place drips with religion."

Modern Precept for Promotion: "Persistence is a key to realizing ambitions."

"Spare your benefactors."

The Hart and the Vine

Hunters chased Hart who hid in vines rude.
Hart would have been safe in shelter crude,
Except the greedy beast
Ate leaves in thoughtless feast,
Was seen and shot for ingratitude.

Aesop's Moral: "Spare your benefactors."

The Contemporary Illustration

The Rape of the Land became an instant best seller when it was published. The book raised two questions immediately. First, who had written the expose? The publisher frankly stated on the dust jacket that the name credited with the authorship was pseudonymous for protection against retaliation. But that question was secondary in importance to another: What would American General Corporation, the giant conglomerate in lumber, land development, mining and housing, do about the charges made in the book? Or conversely, what would be done to American General as a result of the charges?

Hastings, the vice president for community and public relations, faced the worst crisis in his two years on the job. As usual, he called in Reggie V., his manager of public relations.

"Christ, what a mess!" he was saying before Reggie even could get settled in the leather chair opposite his giant mahogany desk. "Everybody in the damn executive office is climbing the walls. We have to find who did this. And if that's not bad enough we have to do some PR thing to offset *Rape*. The legal eagles are considering a libel suit against the publisher."

"Have we got any grounds?" Reggie examined his fingernails as though they could answer his question.

"I haven't a clue, but everybody thinks some insider must have at least fed information to the author if an insider didn't write it himself. There's stuff in the book that no one could otherwise know. For example, all that background about the Nevada land deals and all that scoop about the president's daughter. Hell, you know the agonies we went through keeping *that* out of the papers. You yourself handled that one — and a damn good job you did on it, too, as I've told you before."

Reggie nodded slightly. "But this is a different horse now. We can't keep *Rape* out of the papers. We won't squelch this. Don't the top boys realize that?"

"Of course," said Hastings. "Nevertheless, they want us to do something — God knows what. Any ideas?" The vice president looked out the window as though he might find some there.

"Only if we can disprove the book's charges." Reggie leaned forward. "The legal people have got to give us the ammunition for a rebuttal. We can't just make up something out of whole cloth."

"One thing that occurred to me," said Hastings, "was to attack the stuff on the president's daughter. Invasion of privacy . . . persecution of an innocent girl . . . the daughter's troubles had nothing to do with American General — that sort of thing."

"Innocent girl, hell!" Reggie turned in his chair angrily. "Ran away from boarding school. Out-and-out prostitute. Three arrests for that. Suspected drug addict. If we hadn't sneaked her into that Swiss sanitarium, she would be in that federal narcotics place in Lexington, Kentucky. We can't use her."

Hastings waved his hands vaguely. "OK, OK. The innocent girl bit is out, but how about invasion of privacy and no connection with American General?"

"But there is a connection," Reggie said with exasperation. "*Rape* makes the point that the president used American General's prestige and power to hush the whole thing up."

"You've read the book?" asked Hastings in surprise.

"Of course, haven't you?"

Hastings had not, but Reggie had — if only because he had written it.

How and why do some people turn on their employer on whom they depend for a living? Psychologists, theorists and the employing benefactors themselves have puzzled over this for decades. Many explanations for the "how" of the phenomenon have surfaced, but these stand out:

1. A series of frustrations almost always sets the psychological climate that makes the betrayal ultimately possible.

Ten years earlier, fresh from a reporting job on a metropolitan daily, Reggie had joined as a public relations specialist a company that became the nucleus of American General. At first, he had risen rapidly as the conglomerate expanded and as his own experience broadened. But two years ago his progress had stopped abruptly with the arrival of Hastings from a firm American General had acquired in a stock transfer deal. As Reggie pieced the story together, Hastings had been the major stockholder in the firm and emerged as a holder of a respectable number of American General shares. In addition, he had wrangled as part of the deal a vice presidency in the parent company, which turned out to be the position Reggie thought he should have had.

Besides being thwarted in his ambition, Reggie considered Hastings incompetent and lazy.

2. One particularly disagreeable event — often trivial in itself and perhaps even irrelevant — triggers the event of the betrayal.

The case of the president's daughter proved the last straw for Reggie. He had performed as the good soldier and kept the scandal out of the press. But his disgust grew both at the episode itself and at the squandered credibility he had to suffer with his news sources to keep the matter quiet.

3. The betrayer always rationalizes his action as a minor move or as some noble cause.

Reggie tried both routes. Because he was familiar with publishing (American General had recently acquired a publisher), he knew that most new books sink without a trace. On the one hand, he rationalized that his book would suffer the common fate and be scarcely noticed. Yet, he would still have done his duty, supported the noble cause, by at least trying to expose what he saw as skull-duggery.

4. Results of betrayal are often unexpectedly dramatic and far-reaching.

Betrayers from Judas on down have discovered this to their sorrow. *Rape's* immediate success had even surprised its publisher (whom Reggie had found through a friend at American General's new acquisition). The PR manager, on the other hand, didn't know whether to be appalled or delighted. From a sales standpoint, the book's timing had been ideal, to hit the crest of the ecology "crisis" with a backstage story of a glamourous conglomerate whose well-publicized motto was "the ecology company" — ironically, one of Reggie's contributions.

As to the "why" of treason, psychologists claim that some people are bad psychological employment risks because they are betrayal-prone. First, they tend to believe that uninterrupted job progress is their birthright. Reggie believed this. At thirty-six, he had a responsible job and was well paid. Yet that counted for nothing because his progress had stopped.

Second, betrayal-prone people don't want to be indebted to anyone. Reggie felt this way. He didn't want to be indebted to American General. Now that he thought the company had treated him badly, he felt he could pay off his indebtedness.

Third, betrayal-prone people are gamblers at heart and believe in luck. In his subconscious, he knew that he had been lucky to advance as rapidly as he had. He resented that his luck had run out. He railed at the company for turning his good luck sour.

Fourth, a betrayal-prone individual often experiences a love-hate relationship with his benefactor. For years, Reggie had suffered from this ambivalence. He admired American General for its economic success and its spectacular wheeling and dealing. But as he learned more about its methods, his doubts from a social viewpoint had mounted. In the end, he didn't know what his attitude toward his employer was or even should be.

Actually, the best-selling phase of *The Rape of the Land* proved short-lived, as Reggie with his experience in public relations should have predicted. Within a month, the book had dropped from the best-selling lists and from the major columnists' commentaries.

If Reggie could have been the completely objective professional, he would have advised doing little or nothing as the safest PR strategy. "Our counsel are weighing the legal alternatives open to us, and we must hold off commenting on the issue until they have reached a decision," is the most stifling response possible to reporters' inquiries.

Even if he could have been objective, Reggie probably could not have staved off his employer from demanding more than the "lawyers won't let us talk" line. So, he launched a "we will sue for libel" press campaign that succeeded chiefly in keeping the issue alive for a month instead of the more normal two weeks. It also probably sold another ten thousand copies of *Rape,* to provide an extra financial cushion in royalties for the author. That proved fortunate because American General soon discovered the author's identity.

Unknown to Reggie, a team of high-priced private detectives had started work on that question at the very start. Twenty-seven days after *Rape's* publication, they had tapped Reggie as the culprit. He resigned on the twenty-eighth day. The revelation kept the matter in the newspapers for two or three days more. The publisher wanted to launch Reggie on an author's tour, but he had sickened of the whole thing by this time. He now felt more like a paroled convict than the embattled champion of a noble cause.

Although cooler heads prevailed at American General and the company filed no libel charges against Reggie or the publisher, neither did anyone else pick up the gauntlet against American General. One ecology group that had expressed interest grew distracted by a giant oil spill off New Jersey's coast, and another offered to press charges if Reggie would underwrite legal costs. Nothing came from Reggie's calls on federal and state agencies.

So after six months, Reggie began looking for a PR job in industry. Although he could discover no obvious signs of the blackball, he landed nothing. He finally settled in a low-paying job as publicist for the ecology group that had wanted him to finance legal costs. Accepting the likelihood that industry had closed the door on him, he began a new expose about his post-*Rape* experiences.

Reggie never could separate the merits of his ecological case against American General from the fact of his betrayal. The truth was that he had exposed facts through disloyalty. He had committed a moral or ethical crime in the eyes of many employers. Just as many employers show no enthusiasm for hiring known ex-convicts, they expressed similar reluctance to hire a betrayer.

As one employment interviewer candidly explained, "How do we know you won't nail us just like American General the first time you get mad at us?"

"But I assume you are honest and above-board," said Reggie in rebuttal.

"We hope we are, but perhaps American General is too. I've heard no charges being filed against them."

Reggie had tried to smile. "I won't argue that point here, but I assure you I don't get mad at honesty."

"Nonsense," said the interviewer. "Honesty makes some people madder than anything else."

After that exchange, Reggie had quit job hunting in industry. He did not make good progress with his second expose. He abandoned it after he discovered that to seek revenge is to corrode your soul. He had better success with a volume on how industry can contribute to a better ecology.

Modern Precept for Promotion: "Disloyalty will handicap job advancement as fast as anything."

"The gods help those who help
themselves."

Hercules and the Wagoner

His wheels mired, the Wagoner said,
"Oh, God, Please aid me; I'm beat dead."
But Hercules just laughed,
"I am too understaffed,
So just help yourself first instead."

Aesop's Moral: "The gods help those who help themselves."

The Contemporary Illustration

The dictionary defines a patron as a benefactor or anyone who sup-
ports, protects or champions. The patron turns up frequently in situations involving promotions to better jobs. Many people think they need
one or at least would like to have one to advance their careers, as we
have seen in several of the cases examined thus far.

For example, Harvey B., the dilettante assistant furniture buyer in the
fable of the "Hare and the Tortoise", thought the store's chief furniture
buyer was in his corner, but he discovered too late that he was not.

So, the first rule about patronage is: Make sure your patron will really
support, protect and champion you.

If you aren't reasonably certain of him as a benefactor, take care that
you don't pin too many hopes upon him. Harv had misread the chief
buyer's routine comradeship as privileged treatment. This kind of misin-
terpretation is as common as faulty weather forecasts, so double check
your readings. Is your patron's apparent regard for you something special or mere social affability? Has he specifically supported you in the
past in important ways? Why does he champion you? What good will
support of you do him?

Objective answers to these questions might have revealed to Harvey
that the chief buyer did not give him special treatment. He played buddy
to all the buyers, not just Harvey. Furthermore, he was retiring. It
couldn't matter to him who got the job because his career, at least with
that employer, had ended. So, his recommendation could be completely objective. And Harv might have suspected that he was not the

prime candidate if he, in turn, had been objective (which he was far from being).

Yet the chief buyer proved a poor benefactor for an even more fundamental reason: His patronage didn't count for much. The president, not the chief buyer, made the decision on the buyers. Although he courteously asked the retiring man for suggestions, he didn't even follow his recommendations.

Thus, the second rule about patronage is: Make sure your patron can do you some good.

Where does he fit in the power structure? If he won't be your new boss, can he influence the one who would be? What's his own future with the employer?

If you can't answer these questions from your own preceptions and experience (if, for example, you don't know the benefactor well), ask discreet questions. Harv, of course, had no such excuses. He had known the chief buyer for years, but didn't realize the limits of his influence.

People can also serve as poor patrons in other ways. Familiar with dozens is Sidney K., who made extensive use of benefactors throughout his career (in the "Blind Men and the Elephant").

"But the overriding one is exaggeration," he says. "Some people get an ego-kick out of being a patron. To impress their protégés, they may inflate their own importance or the extent of their inside knowledge. Although often harmless, that trait may result in misinformation or poor signals to the protégé.

So, the third rule about patronage is: Make sure your patron is effective.

Does he tend to exaggerate in ways not related to the current situation? If so, watch out that he doesn't also inflate the facts or evaluations concerning your promotion. Has he had a string of protégés over the years — and what has happened to them? If he has had many and if most of them have disappeared, watch out. Does he contact you more than you do him? If so, that's another indication that he wants protégés. In the patron-protégé situation, the petitioner should take the initiative, not vice versa.

Nor can a patron be effective if he's dishonest. In the fable of "Belling the Cat," Walt R., the supposed patron, used Tom Y. to further his own ambitions, not to advance those of his young protégé. The outcome resulted in Tom's getting fired and Walt's continued stalemate in his own career.

The fourth rule, therefore, about patronage is: Make certain that balanced self-interest exists in the patron-protégé relationship.

Don't be surprised if self-interest surfaces somewhere in most patronage situations. This is natural and seldom leads to trouble unless the mutual self-interest slips grossly out of balance, as in the case of Walt and Tom.

Patronage goes awry for other reasons, too. For example, Irving H. underestimated the importance of the family feud (in the "Blind Men and the Elephant"), so George E. took a new job that turned out to be another dead end. At least, that's the way George saw it. Irving, on the other hand, pointed out that he had warned George about the danger of the feud, but George had chosen to ignore the risk.

The fifth rule, then, about patronage is: Make effective use of your patron.

Both Irving and George were at fault in their situation, but George probably more so because he was the supplicant. The petitioner takes the greater risk and should know it. He is the buyer — caveat emptor!

On the other hand, Frank L. and Ray W. mutually used patronage with great effectiveness (in the "Dog in the Manger") when the former first served as patron for the latter and much later when the two reversed roles successfully.

Ed J. also used his patron effectively (in "Belling the Cat" and other fables) by enlisting an acquaintance, not a close friend, to intercede for him with a vice president to become his statistical analyst. Frequently, you will be wiser to choose an acquaintance than a friend as go-between because friendship sometimes distorts judgments. Furthermore, you may lose a friend if you ask him to become your patron.

Not everyone likes patronage, viewing it as ethically or morally wrong. Yet patronage is support, encouragement or championship. Most ethical and moral teachers endorse, don't condemn, such concepts.

When you examine the successful examples of patronage — in the cases of Ed, Frank, and Ray — they all possess these characteristics:

1. There is mutual respect.
2. There is good will.
3. There is honest and balanced self-interest.
4. There is initiative, primarily on the supplicant's part.
5. There is serendipity.

These last two related points need elaboration. All petitioners for aid seek to help themselves, of course. But this tactic seldom succeeds unless the patron will benefit, too. Ed's acquaintance who helped him get a job with a vice president turned out to be less disinterested than first appearances indicated. He was a manpower specialist and had been asked by the vice president, to whom he reported, to find a statistical analyst for him. Ed's petition came along shortly after the acquaintance had received the charge. Blind luck? No, it's serendipity.

The word was coined by Horace Walpole in 1754 to denote the faculty of happening upon or making fortunate discoveries when not in search of the specific development. But people who experience serendipity invariably are searching for something. They have already taken the initiative.

Frank helped Ray early in the latter's career. Then Ray returned the favor years later when Frank had grown restless over his current situation and had told Ray about it at lunch which the two friends continued to have periodically. As it happened, Ray had an opening that suited Frank. That was serendipity again, not blind luck. Some might even call it the work of the gods.

Modern Precept for Promotion: "Promotion comes when it mutually benefits both patron and protégé."

"Advantages may be dearly bought."

Horse and Man

The proud Horse let the Man on his back.
"We will fill," said Man, "each other's lack."
Yet the partners fell out,
Horse wanted the hell out.
But Man made him his slave and his hack.

Aesop's Moral: "Advantages may be dearly bought."

The Contemporary Illustration

ABC Products, Inc. did a solid business in metal stampings and plastic parts — 1,000 employees, $35 million in annual sales and $2.5 million in after-tax profits.

Oscar O. had sold successfully for ABC over nearly three decades. Several years earlier he had led a campaign by other salesmen and some of the engineering people to diversify into plastics, and his argument had been, "If you can't beat them, join them." The move had helped revitalize ABC which had been fighting a losing battle against the competitive inroads from the material.

Oscar had made himself an expert on it and had become the company's leading salesman for plastics which now accounted for almost half its volume.

So, when ABC's sales manager died of a heart attack at fifty-eight, no one was surprised that Oscar succeeded him. Least of all, Oscar.

"Frankly, I would have quit if they had picked someone else," he told his wife at a celebration dinner.

"Yes, but how are you going to like all the desk work?" she had asked.

"I'm going to run this job differently." He waved his hand expansively. "There's been too much paper work. The sales manager's got to get out into the field more. I've said this all along."

"I thought you didn't like it when Chris went with you on trips." She looked at him reflectively over the brim of a champagne glass. "You called it meddling."

"What Chris did was meddling. I'm going to do it to support the guys in the field."

"How?"

"I'm going to concentrate on new business — new customers, new uses for our products, maybe even new products."

"Yes, but you've always said that you couldn't stand a desk job."

"Honey, it won't be a desk job, the way I handle it."

She still looked troubled. "Did you tell them that?"

"I told them how I planned to handle the job. They didn't object. Come on Honey, this is a celebration, not a wake."

She forced a smile. "Of course, you know me, always the worrier."

His smile was more genuine. "Think of the money this promotion will bring — at least 20 per cent more. Besides, you don't want me to stick as just a road runner for the rest of my life, do you? The only promotion open to me in this outfit was the sales managership. It was the only way up."

She frowned again. "But we don't really need the money. The kids are all through college and doing well. You were earning plenty."

Oscar raised his hands in mock despair. "That's funny coming from you. Who frets and stews over the bills each month? Who fusses that we never can save any money? Well, now we can. We'll put some away for retirement. After all, that's only about a dozen years away."

So, they continued their muted celebration, and she voiced no more disquieting thoughts. As they were going to bed later, he added one of his own, although he had meant it to be reassuring. "You know, you got to do some things sometimes just to find out if you can do them. I'd never know if I would make a good sales manager unless I tried it, would I?"

She changed the subject.

In Oscar's first three months on the job, he had to go on the road a lot, but not to develop new business. Rather, it was to save several accounts they already had. A flurry of missed delivery dates and poor quality had resulted in four good customers threatening to buy elsewhere. He had to journey to each of them for time-consuming "hand-holding" sessions, and he had to spend more hours in the shop with manufacturing and engineering people to get at the source of the problems.

Furthermore, he had to reinstate several sales reports, which he had abolished, because their absence had left him not realizing until the eleventh hour that ABC had problems with the four customers. He saved the business, but at the cost of much expenditure in time and nervous energy. He found himself putting in twelve-hour days, and he began to suffer insomnia, a malady which had never troubled him before.

After six months on the job, Oscar caught a heavy cold that he couldn't throw off. It evolved into pneumonia, and he ended up in the hospital for the first time since his birth.

At his bedside, his wife said, "Oscar, when you recover from this, I want you to give thought to resigning the sales managership."

"I can't do that." He waved an arm weakly. "I've only been on the job six months. I haven't had time to give it a fair trial. Besides, where could I go if I stopped being sales manager? I couldn't go back to just selling. And that's all there is for me at ABC."

"Couldn't the company create a new job for you in sales development? You've always said they needed someone for that."

Oscar turned over, not facing her. "ABC is too small to support that kind of a job. Only the big outfits can carry the overhead."

"Well, then, why not try for such a job with a larger company?"

"Honey!" He turned again to face her. "I've been with ABC twenty-eight years! Throw all that away — the pension, everything?"

She leaned forward. "You wouldn't be throwing it away. Couldn't you keep what you've already contributed toward the pension and what the company has contributed, too? There's some name for that."

"Vesting — and I don't have it with ABC. If I leave ABC before I am sixty for any reason, all I get back is the money I've contributed — none of ABC's contribution. And I'm seven years away from being sixty."

"I know. But you could be just weeks or months from being on this earth at all if you continue like this."

They were both silent. He attempted a laugh, but it came out as a croak. "Come on now, it's not as bad as all that."

"The doctor says it is, Oscar. I've been talking to him. Darling, this is serious. I want you to leave the job."

Many circumstances arise in a person's career where advantages may be dearly bought, but three stand out:

1. When you over-mortgage your future for present gains. In the "Goose with the Golden Eggs," we have already seen what may happen if you do that.

2. When you assume too high a risk of failure. The fable of the "Geese and the Cranes" illustrates the danger of that course.

3. When you accept the wrong promotion, as in Oscar's case.

Oscar faced a problem common in career advancement — the correct path for the future isn't available with your present employer. As Oscar did, you accept what's available even though you have misgivings about your decision.

Although Oscar had more doubts from the start than he admitted to his wife, ABC's president had overridden them.

"Of course you can handle the job, Oscar," he had said. "You know this company like the back of your hand. You know our products, and you have done a fine job getting us into plastics." The president had endorsed Oscar's proposal to reduce paper work and had been enthusiastic about his ideas on sales development. So, he had persuaded Oscar to take the job against his better judgment. Thus, the first requirement to avoid taking the road to a career disaster lies in resisting the efforts of others to lure you into a wrong career path. This happens usually when the employer finds himself with an unexpected job opening which he must — or at least believes he must — fill at once. He tends to pick the most obvious choice — the Oscars of the world.

Of course, you must know your own abilities, and that's not as easy as it sounds, as noted in the "Fox and the Grapes." This is the second "must" to avoid the wrong promotion. As Oscar said to his wife, it is difficult to know what you can do until you try it. You can get an advance idea, however, from your own inclinations, experiences and wishes. If you must try a career course that may prove a poor route, do it as early as possible. Unfortunately, Oscar never had tried managing before in all his years of selling.

Sometimes you can test yourself briefly by substituting for a man whose job you might like while he's on vacation or is absent for other reasons. Oscar's manager rarely went on extended vacation, taking odd days here and there instead. So, Oscar never could test the water that way until the manager died prematurely of a heart attack. To prepare yourself better than Oscar did, therefore, you should experiment early with various job alternatives — the third safeguard against the wrong career choice.

The fourth method to keep yourself on the track lies in analyzing the opportunities available with your employer. What can he offer? Does anything suit you? Will he present such chance to you within a reasonable time? If the employer can't offer you what you want, leave him, and do it soon. Ideally, Oscar should have departed from ABC years earlier, to find an employer large enough to support a sales development staff.

Smaller companies normally can offer significant promotions only through the managerial ranks. They aren't large enough to support any or many individual contributors. If your abilities lie in the individual contributing area, be sure your employer has sufficient opportunities here. ABC, on a formal basis, offered only the conventional selling job to the individual contributor.

Now Oscar didn't want to return to that — a not uncommon phenomenon. A person who is reasonably content in one job, gets promoted but returns to the former position, often finds that the old job no longer gives him satisfaction. A "sea change" occurs frequently in this circumstance.

The fifth way of assuring yourself the proper promotion is to find an employer that offers the kind of job you want. Although this seems obvious, it needs mention because many people find their career stymied for this reason alone.

When Oscar emerged from the hospital, he had decided to leave ABC. Luckily, the company's president proved sympathetic. He decided the firm had grown large enough now to support a sales development specialist. Oscar moved to that new position and eventually found it rewarding from both the standpoints of career satisfaction and compensation.

Modern Precept for Promotion: "Not every promotion may be worth the price you pay for it."

"Laziness is its own punishment."

The Lazy Housemaids

Two Maids killed the rooster whose loud bawl
Roused Mistress at first dawn, to their gall.
    Now they're more furious
    Because — it's curious —
She's up even earlier to call.

Aesop's Moral: "Laziness is its own punishment."

The Contemporary Illustration

Ursula P. made numerous trips to the ladies' room, took an hour and a half for lunch frequently and had two or three sick days each month that fell either on Monday or Friday.

Her boss tolerated her because her secretarial skills were good when she chose to exercise them. Yet when she missed three successive Mondays, even he grew impatient and called her in for a talk.

"What seems to be the trouble?" he asked.

"I'm worrying myself sick," she replied. "My worrying seems to get worse on weekends, and that's why I'm sick on Mondays."

"What are you worrying about?"

"My job. I don't seem to be getting anywhere in it. Girls who joined the company about the same time I did get promoted, but I don't."

Her boss cleared his throat. "About four or five months ago, you'll remember, we had a talk about promotion possibilities. Remember what I said about improving your application?"

"Yes, and I have improved it. I'm trying harder, but it doesn't do any good."

Ursula's boss sent her to the company's psychologist whose report on her started with three words, "Ursula is lazy." The boss's first reaction was disbelief. In this age of permissiveness nobody's simply lazy; there's an underlying reason for laziness — emotional handicaps, economic disadvantages, personal troubles — as any psychologist should know. But psychologists themselves are beginning to question that deeper maladies *always* underlie laziness. While some people are disadvantaged or emotionally handicapped, others don't like to work. That alone is their problem.

Professor James L. Windle, a member of Purdue University's Department of Industrial Supervision, says: "Work by definition is labor, exertion and toil. Some people like to work, and, too, some workers like routine and dislike responsibilities; some have low ability; some are lazy."

The psychologist who saw Ursula learned that she liked to type but disliked to file or keep records. He suggested that she get as much typing as possible. Because the job entailed little typing and lots of filing and record keeping, those suggestions weren't too useful. The boss sent her back to the typing pool, thinking that she would quit over this indignity. Ursula did not; she was too lazy to look for another job.

Vance U. didn't seem lazy. From his desk flowed a stream of memos. He was the office's champion FYI man, constantly circulating to peers and superiors Xeroxed copies of articles from newspapers and magazines "for your information." However, he wrote few reports and research papers himself, having a consummate skill in maneuvering others to do the work for him. As a consultant on communication to a vice president, nobody knew for what or to whom exactly he had responsibility. So his colleagues tended to play it safe. Although they grumbled, they wrote the report that Vance said "JSM suggested." JSM, of course, was the vice president.

Vance used another ploy, too. He had access to reports prepared by other components in the organization. He chaired "study teams" to evaluate the reports "from our own perspectives." The team members each wrote evaluations and Vance "synthesized" them into one evaluation that presumably went to JSM. Nobody ever heard of the report or the evaluation again.

But the best weapon in Vance's arsenal was work plans. At the start of each year, he devised them — but always for others to implement. Coupled with this was Vance's responsibility which he had somehow acquired for work measurement. He kept score on the implementation and provided a quarterly accounting to JSM, together with new plans if the schedule had gone awry. When it did go awry, as frequently happened, he wrote lengthy memos to the culprit, with a carbon to JSM, outlining the methods for "corrective action."

The memos, FYI Xeroxed copies, study teams, work plans and measurement activity kept Vance so busy that he didn't notice the troops' restiveness. They nominated three of their members to air their grievances against Vance to JSM. As the vice president listened, he grew increasingly attentive. He had thought the FYI thing and the elaborate work plan and measurement activity were cumbersome holdovers from his predecessor's days, and he had been reluctant to drop them.

He was particularly indignant over the evaluation study teams. He had not known of their existence and had merely asked Vance to "look over" the reports, thinking that the evaluations were the consultant's own work, although unnecessarily thorough.

Vance soon left the vice president as his communication consultant, but he landed at least on one foot elsewhere in the organization as manager of the mailroom. There, too, his busyness masked his fundamental problem — laziness, or a reluctance to do meaningful work.

Busyness isn't the only way to mask a reluctance to do meaningful work. Dilettantism proves a handy shield, too. Harvey B., the assistant furniture buyer whom we met in the "Hare and the Tortoise," pursued his calling in a desultory and superficial way — the dictionary's definition for dilettantism. This helped assure that Connie S., who had been working as an assistant buyer for a much shorter time than he, easily surpassed him and became the senior buyer.

Martin V., however, was neither a dilettante like Harvey, nor a busywork phony like Vance, nor a malingerer like Ursula. He disarmingly admitted his laziness, to the extent that people thought him amusing or a fellow who chose to mask his diligence behind a facade of insouciance.

As a staff man for a large government agency responsible for the organization's manpower planning, he could get away with a certain amount of laziness. Nobody knew exactly what he did, including at first the agency's head, a recent appointee from a large university. Martin's most urgent responsibility was to staff the top twenty jobs in the agency with reasonably competent and attractive people. To this task, Martin devoted most of his energies and discharged his duties to most people's satisfaction. But a vacancy occurred among this score of positions only once or twice a year (about double that rate, perhaps, when a new administration came in, but this could not happen more often than once every four years).

Martin spent much time on the phone, presumably talking with his "contacts," attending numerous personnel conferences to "keep abreast of things," and going to many big scientific association meetings "to keep in touch with the field" because his agency had as its main function the funneling of government-developed technology into the private sector.

Out of these travels and conversations came a monthly newsletter, an ad hoc thing that he called "Martin's Memo" circulated among the agency's key people. It was a compendium of gossip about agency alumni, amusing anecdotes about his misadventures and even occasionally some hard news about the agency's manpower changes and other developments. This last had been the original justification for the "Memo" years before, but now it read more like the class notes in a college alumni magazine. Indeed, it was no accident that Martin did write such notes for his own class in his college's alumni magazine. Frequently, the tales of misadventures appeared in both places.

Jokes (sample — subject of my master's thesis: "What College Done for Me") and stories of difficulties with his golf score that appeared in "Martin's Memo" contributed to his reputation as a wit and a delight. Surely, such a fellow would not goof off. But he did, as the former university man who now headed the agency eventually established to his own satisfaction. Martin was nowhere to be found at a personnel conference in Chicago where the agency boss fruitlessly had tried to reach him for three days. Although Martin had a civil service rating and could not easily be fired, his boss had him shunted to the watchdog agency, the most unpopular organization in all of government.

Modern Precept for Promotion: "Keeping a good job requires hard work; getting a better one demands even harder effort."

"You can't hope to please all; don't try."

The Man That Pleased None

Dad rode donkey — to jeers en masse.
Son took a turn — scorn from a lass.
They both rode — no applause.
The beast rode them — haw-haws.
Then donkey fell — they'd lost their ass.

Aesop's Moral: "You can't hope to please all; don't try."

The Contemporary Illustration

Although you can't hope to please all, you want to please as many as reasonably possible.

Florence E. ran one of the most potentially troublesome units in the company, the office typing pool. But it ran smoothly, and many "graduates" of the pool eventually landed top secretarial jobs with the firm's executives.

"One of the keys to success in a pool operation," she says, "is to offer the girls in it hope of advancement. This I do through my 'graduate' program. In this headquarters office alone, we have nearly a hundred private secretarial jobs. I took this position with the understanding that my qualified girls would have the opportunity to fill every opening. Almost once per month, there's an opportunity, so we get lots of movement upward."

But Florence had more than this going for her. She headed off complaints before they arose by keeping an eye on potential trouble spots, by being fair and patient, even with chronic gripers, by being honest and giving the full story, and by giving advance notice of change.

No wonder that Florence eventually won promotion to a newly created position as a consultant on office practices for the entire company — advising headquarters and all field offices on how to deal more effectively with clerical help.

Yet, human nature being what it is, some complaints are still inevitable. Florence's advice: "Expect them; take them in stride. Don't let them unduly upset you."

Complaints will come from three principal sources: outsiders, employees and the boss.

Asa A. had fought a losing battle to keep his drop-forging plant going. It failed, however. You would have thought its demise would have pleased at least one person, a housewife whose home adjoined the noisy forging plant who had long fought its presence. Besides complaining about the din and dirt, she didn't like the employees' boisterous and blasphemous talk when they ate lunch outside during nice weather. When management got the men to moderate their voices and language, she complained about employees parking their cars in front of her house. When parking places were found elsewhere, she demanded that management plant a thick high row of evergreens along the mutual property line. When the plant went out of business, she protested as loudly as anyone — her teenage son had just entered the labor market and had lost a potential employer.

The more people you have to please, the less chance for success. Since more outsiders exist than insiders, you're bound to miss with some. The most common complaining group among outsiders will be customers. Deal with their gripes seriously and promptly.

Most of the grievances you receive will come from your own people. If your plant is organized by a labor union, your contract probably has an established procedure for dealing with them. There's no need to go into that here because the mechanics vary. Anyhow, mechanics aren't as important as the human relations you use to deal with the gripes.

An employee in an automotive parts plant complained of the noise his machine made and suggested a muffling device to lower the decibel level. Kermit F., his supervisor, had heard many complaints about the noise, and he acted upon this one as he had with all the others — by doing nothing.

He explained that he realized that the noise level was somewhat high, but that others had found it bearable and that anyone who really wanted to work there could find the situation livable.

Another employee complained to Kermit that a casting was too heavy for one man to lift comfortably.

"I lifted it easily when I had your job," said Kermit in dismissing the complaint.

Still another griped about the odors in the plant, claiming they made him sick.

"I don't smell anything," said Kermit, pretending to sniff the air like a dog.

In still another case, the beleaguered Kermit thought he had resolved a grievant's complaint about incentive rates. He got new ones established which supposedly met all the objections, but unbeknown to him, the grievant got transferred to another machine and lost his hard-won gains.

Poor Kermit! He went out of his way to make sure that he pleased nobody, which is as shortsighted as trying to please everybody.

Kermit failed in four of the five basic rules about dealing with grievances when they do arise:

1. Listen as objectively and imaginatively as possible to the complainer. Kermit listened to only half of the gripe about the noise, ignoring the concrete suggestion for changing the equipment. He had heard the noise grievance so often that custom deafened him to the other part of the proposition. "Pay careful attention," cautions Florence, "to those complaints accompanied by remedies. Usually the solution is impractical, but every once in a while it works. Many grievances can lead to improvements in the way to do the job, or in actions that management can take. The key is to handle all complaints objectively, as if you are hearing them for the first time."

2. Investigate the charges. When the employee challenged Kermit to lift the heavy casting, the supervisor discovered to his embarrassment that it required more effort than he had remembered exerting years earlier.

3. Promise remedy if the grievant is right. Determining this sometimes proves difficult. In the case about the odors, Kermit honestly could detect nothing — literally that is. But something else underlay that complaint, and Kermit should have smelled it out. The grievant really disliked a fellow employee and wanted to get transferred to some other job. He hated to give the real reason for his wish and touched on just one of many things he found objectionable working next to the other — the fellow's strong body odor. If Kermit had probed deeper, he might have uncovered the real problem. Florence comments: "It takes psychological skill and courage to determine whether the apparent grievance is the real one."

4. Follow through. Kermit didn't do so in the incentive rate example. The employee who was shifted to another machine interpreted the transfer as a Machiavellian plot to "cheat" him after he had won a significant victory. If Kermit had followed up quickly, he would have discovered the happenstance and could have set matters right. Instead, the employee suffered in silence for a while, working up a monumental rage that we'll hear more about shortly. Florence's advice in a situation like this: "Face up to the problem that you may have caused in whole or in part. In these cases, the grievant may not speak up at all or not until the eleventh hour. Then the trouble is that much worse because time needed for the remedy may have nearly run out."

5. Hold firm if no remedy is justified. Kermit did this well, but he too often goofed with the first four rules and didn't always know when no remedy was justified. Disaster will eventually follow if you try to ap-

pease a complainer, especially if you suspect the charge is trumped up or erroneous. Proof of this lies in history, notably in the attempts to appease Hitler just before World War II. If you aren't going to do anything about an unjustified grievance, say so. Never let it go without comment. If the patient merely suffers from hypochondria, a blunt statement to that effect often proves the only remedy.

Although Kermit gave short shrift to many of his employees' complaints, he awarded close attention to most everything his boss, the plant manager, had to say. Often he over-reacted, a common failing that I'll·deal with in the fuller discussion about how to cope with your boss in the fable of the "Ox and the Axletrees."

The day came when Kermit's manager did want a fast reaction. The complainer who had the idea about a noise muffler for his machine came directly to the manager with his proposal. It intrigued the manager and he grew disturbed to learn that Kermit had done nothing about it.

"I looked the drawings over," said Kermit in defense of himself, "and didn't see much in them. Maybe I brushed the idea off too fast, but this guy's a chronic bellyacher. Frankly, he kinda burns me up."

The manager sighed. "Polodsky has an idea that's worth looking into more deeply, I think. Get the engineering people on it now."

"Yessir," said Kermit, scooping up the drawings and ready to leave as rapidly as possible.

"Just a minute, Kermit. There's something even more serious that's come up. Latimer came in yesterday and has a pretty serious charge. He claims you corrected his incentive rate and then promptly moved him to another machine. The dirtiest trick ever pulled on him here, he says."

"What? Latimer's crazy. He's still on that machine."

"No, he was pulled off right after the new rate became effective. I know because I checked with Billings."

Kermit pounded his fist on the boss's desk. "Billings! He's done it again. Shifting people around without checking it out with me."

"Do you require that Billings check these moves out with you?"

"Yes, you're damn right!"

"Billings says that's news to him. He says you don't want to be bothered with every little change."

"That's a damn lie! Wait until I see Billings."

"We'll see him now — both of us."

There followed a confrontation so painful to Kermit that he thought he would be fired on the spot. Three days later when he was called to the manager's office, he went with some trepidation.

The boss was all business. "The engineers like this muffler idea and think it can be installed for only about $100. We're going to do it."

"Yes sir. I think it's a fine proposal, too."

"You didn't think that three days ago."

"No, I made a mistake there."

"You certainly did. And you made mistakes with Latimer and with Billings. I think we've had enough mistakes around here, don't you?"

Kermit shifted uneasily. "Yes. There will be no more, if I have anything to do with it."

The manager looked out the window. "Kermit, you're not going to have anything more to do with it. I'm relieving you of the supervisory job. Billings will take your place. You can have your old job back on the machine."

Kermit stood up as he muttered, "I don't want that. I quit."

Modern Precept for Promotion: "You can't please everybody, but you had better please those who count."

"One may be too ambitious."

The Married Mouse

Mister Mouse took Miss Lion as bride.
Very great was his joy and his pride.
But it chanced that she put
On her husband her foot
And the weight was so great that he died.

Aesop's Moral: "One may be too ambitious."

The Contemporary Illustration

Calvin M.'s resume is impressive. Upon graduation with a journalism degree from Northwestern, he joined a Chicago-based trade magazine. Within two years, he had moved to a New York-headquartered consumer magazine in the housing field. He left that post three years later for a land development company. That ended in only eighteen months because of "an offer too good to pass up to rejoin the consumer magazine as managing editor," according to the resume. But that publication changed ownership within two years, and Cal "chose not to accept the new owner's employment offer, to go into business for myself as a consultant to housing supply manufacturers and home builders."

That was a year ago. Now Cal faces the advertising manager for a major company's building products division who seeks to hire a sales promotion specialist. Will he hire this thirty-two-year-old, personable man, obviously knowledgeable about housing and housing products? Cal is asking for $35,000 yearly, higher than what the ad man plans to pay, but still not out of reason.

"What happened to your consulting business?" the manager asks.

"I had the customers," said Cal with a wry grin, "but not the payers." He names one client who recently created business headlines by declaring bankruptcy.

"You mean that just one client's failure did you in?"

"I had others." He names three smaller firms whose names the manager recognizes. "But this was the big one — the one I gave most of my time and energies to. I also had a considerable financial commitment made on their behalf in printing and so on. When they went under, they left me holding the bag."

"Is your firm in bankruptcy, too?"

"Yes." Another wry smile. "I had no other choice."

The two talked some more, but the guts of the job interview had already taken place. Cal had impressed the ad manager, but that veteran's long experience with people — or perhaps just intuition — had sent up danger signals in his mind. He made several telephone calls to old friends in the industry. Within a day, he had heard enough to draw this picture about Calvin, which varied from what had shown on the resume and even from the surface impressions during the job interview:

Cal indeed had a Northwestern journalism degree. He had left the trade magazine in Chicago at the editor's request. The departure wasn't officially listed as discharge, but one step removed. Cal had proved to be an energetic and enterprising reporter — too much so because he had antagonized some of his news sources and all his fellow editors through overaggression.

"He considered everything a contest," the editor recalled, "and every other person on the staff an antagonist. He was impossible on all our numerous team-reporting projects. He created so much dissension that we had to let him go. Too bad. He had the makings of a great reporter."

He fitted better into the New York magazine environment because he had learned a lesson in Chicago and because his brand of aggression was tolerated more in New York. Yet the tolerance didn't extend as far as a fist fight in the office, which precipitated Calvin's first departure from the publication. The battle ostensibly stemmed from a disagreement over credit for authorship of an article, but it went much deeper than that. Calvin considered the other a rival, and antagonism between the two had simmered for months.

The job with a land development firm had served as a stopgap only. Cal had waited until a new man who admired him became the consumer magazine's editor and politicked to get rehired. So anxious was he for reinstatement that he turned a blind eye to signs of trouble on the publication, such as extensive staff turnover. The turnover helped Cal climb rapidly to the managing editorship. He had not gone to that post immediately as implied in the resume.

The facts behind the employment offer by the magazine's new owner were also not quite as implied in the resume. Under the purchase agreement, the new owner had to offer jobs to all the existing staff, but not at their old positions or salaries. Cal had immediately refused a proposal as a reporter at a salary 20 per cent under his former level.

Yet the most telling evidence of excessive ambition surfaced in Cal's career as a consultant.

"We took advantage of the kid, "a survivor from the bankrupt home products company confided to the advertising manager. "And of course we were ripe for this kind of guy — good and cheap. With our money troubles, we had to go for the low dollar. He gave us too much for the money we paid — or rather didn't pay. I feel a little guilty about that, but, hell, it was a gamble and he knew it. It might have paid off for him big."

So, Cal was not quite the innocent victim he had portrayed of the bankrupt client. He had known about the firm's difficulties and had taken it as a client anyway.

Cal's tale illustrates several characteristics of the overly ambitious person:

- He's seldom satisfied, moving frequently from job to job or enterprise to enterprise.
- He usually has many outstanding abilities.
- He usually makes good initial impressions.
- He's ruthless with others to achieve his goals.
- His ambition sometimes clouds his judgment.
- He will readily take risks, sometimes foolish ones.
- He frequently fails in business for himself because of lapses in judgment.
- He has trouble recognizing his ambition as excessive; therefore he sometimes can't curb it.
- He has difficulty working for others, but a strong manager may be able to bring out the best in him.

The advertising manager offered Cal a job at $28,000 per year. He chose that figure because his budget permitted it; because he had learned it was $1,000 above what Cal had earned when he left the consumer magazine; because it was far above the income he had earned during his abortive year as a consultant; and because it would still enable him to award a good raise in about a year if things worked out.

But the ad manager offered a job with strings. He tied the proposal with advice and a proviso. He didn't tell Cal that he had learned some facts that disputed his resume claims. Rather, he flatly told him that he was too ambitious and that this trait had led him into his numerous job changes and into some bad decisions in his consulting work.

"You're going to be on your own here, but responsible to me," he told him. "The sales promotion staff will consist of you and a secretary — no one else. The advertising and employee communication work is performed by others. When you want some legitimate sales promotion work done by the ad or communication people, you work through me. All of your promotional ideas must be submitted to me. The first — repeat first — sign that you are stirring up any discord in my staff or that you have tried to bypass me in any way means your automatic dismissal."

Cal started to protest, but the ad manager interrupted. "I know this sounds tough, and I don't lay down rules like these for everyone. But I believe you're a special case. You're a gifted guy, but you haven't realized anywhere near your potential. You've frittered your opportunities away. I'm giving you the chance to make something of yourself — and to help me too of course. I believe this is the only way we both can achieve something. You can take it or leave it."

Cal took it. Although he went through some difficult times with the manager, he came to recognize that joining with him was the most fortunate thing that had ever happened to his career; because he became the premier sales promotion man in the field.

The ad manager started Cal off on the right foot. First, he isolated him from the rest of his staff to guard against organizational chaos. Second, he managed him with a firmer hand than he did other staff members, because he was error-prone. Third, he praised him lavishly for the many examples of good work that he did. Fourth, he gave him judicious increases in salary periodically. Fifth, he upgraded his job title from time to time — from specialist to consultant to manager for sales promotion.

Cal was fortunate to have a strong and wise manager who channeled his ambitions constructively. Many overly ambitious people find their ambitions eventually crush them.

Modern Precept for Promotion: "You can push too hard to get ahead."

"Don't count your chickens before they
are hatched."

The Milkmaid and Her Pail

Miss Milkmaid's capitalist dreams
Of gains from milk and chicks, it seems,
Lost their supporting legs
'Fore she even bought eggs —
She tripped, to spill her milk in streams.

Aesop's Moral: "Don't count your chickens before they are hatched."

The Contemporary Illustration

Probably the most notorious bit of counting chickens before they were hatched occurred in 1948 when the *Chicago Tribune* committed the offense on Thomas E. Dewey's behalf by prematurely headlining his victory over Harry S. Truman for the U.S. presidency. More seriously, the Dewey campaign staff had thought they would win and had consciously or unconsciously let down and allowed complacency to dominate them.

The unconscious or (more rarely) conscious complacency, of course, is the real danger in your efforts for promotion.

Chuck L. thought he had the general foreman's spot sewed up. He had been the sidekick and confidante of Joe, the retiring general foreman. He had seniority over every other foreman in the shop. When the plant manager said nothing to him about a promotion, he didn't give the oversight a second thought — until one of the other foremen was announced as the successor.

Chuck made several errors, the most serious being the assumption that Joe had recommended him as his successor. Although Joe liked Chuck well enough and occasionally had a beer with him after work, he made a practice of remaining friendly with all the foremen who reported to him. He knew that Chuck assumed he had the job, but Chuck had never asked directly for his recommendation. Such complacency irritated Joe, especially because all the other foremen had asked for his good word.

Chuck had pointedly referred to his own seniority several times, not realizing the extent of Joe's antipathy toward the principle with which the union had plagued him for years.

Chuck's third error was in assuming that Joe had the final word on choosing a successor; a misconception Chuck would have soon discovered if he had ever troubled to discuss the matter with Joe. Joe merely made recommendations to the plant manager. Actually, the plant manager picked Joe's second nominee, not the first. (Joe had placed Chuck third on the slate.)

While Chuck's unconscious complacency contributed to his failure to win a promotion, Bill S.'s conscious complacency nearly did him in.

Bill wanted the engineering managership, but refused to ask for it. "If they don't know I'm the best man for the job without my having to tell them," he said to his wife repeatedly, "I'll quit. I wouldn't want to work for such idiots."

"But honey," his wife would warn, "they may not know you want the job. Can't you at least hint?"

Finally when nothing happened for several weeks, Bill did hint, and a day later he was offered the position. Like the salesman who doesn't get the order because he doesn't ask directly for it, some people don't get promoted because they don't specifically ask for the better job.

A boss often has a problem, too. He wants to avoid the awkwardness of having someone, especially a current employee, refuse a promotion. Many bosses also prefer to promote people who they think are at least a little hungry and ambitious. If the boss can't tell about a candidate, he may pass over him.

This matter of asking for the promotion takes strange forms sometimes. Hal K. wanted to become manager of employee relations. His strategy was to tell the boss he didn't want the job! His reasons for such a course were convoluted, but they had a kind of logic. He didn't think he had much chance for the promotion; even feared he wasn't being considered for it. He thought that he would sound presumptuous if he flatly asked for it. His method of bringing his name to the attention of the boss was to suggest — ever so obliquely — that he didn't want this particular promotion at this time, but that he might want it or something similar later.

Hal's assessment proved only partly accurate; the boss had considered and rejected him for the opening because of inexperience. But Hal's reverse action let the boss know he had ambition. He was destined to get more serious consideration next time.

Far more common is the case of the person who runs too hard for office. Jake R. didn't have a chance of becoming manager for manufacturing because at least two other people were better qualified. Yet he either didn't or couldn't understand this and made an impassioned plea for the promotion. By the time it became clear that someone else would win the job, Jake had worked himself into an untenable position. Although he hadn't meant it to sound so strong, he had left the impression that he would quit if he didn't get promoted. When he didn't resign, the boss had to ask him to do so, reasoning that a man who felt so deeply about the missed promotion could no longer perform effectively on his continuing job.

Simply talking too much among your peers may prove mistaken or at least embarrassing if you don't win the nod. A successful (and therefore promotable) man must retain the ability to generate confidence. You'll do the opposite if you fail to win the job that you have told many colleagues you expect to get. If you haven't discussed the matter, many can assume you did not want to be in the running. Dr. Robert McMurry, the psychologist who heads a Chicago-based management consulting firm, advised an ambitious client: "Always give the impression of knowing what you are doing, even when you are not sure at all." The best way to accomplish this is to make only those who need to know aware of your ambitions — no one else.

In the fable "Belling the Cat," I told about Jack M. who had a job thrust upon him that he neither expected nor wanted. That's a kind of chicken-counting, too. Jack eventually refused the job, after first implying that he accepted it. His better course: To have been prepared for the offer and prepared to refuse it politely and logically on the spot. Jack could be excused for temporizing at first if he had been genuinely surprised that he got the offer. Yet, complete surprise is rare and usually occurs only if you are sleeping at your desk. Even if a promotion seems remote, prepare yourself mentally on how you would respond if lightning does strike.

Another species of chicken-counting occurs in excessive job-hopping — for example, if your resume shows job changes almost annually. While you make most hops because you think the next job amounts to a promotion, the time may come when the next position represents a demotion. Then you will really have counted chickens before they were hatched.

Modern Precept for Promotion: "Don't count on the promotion until you get it locked up."

"Don't make much ado about nothing."

The Mountain in Labor

Mountain did not try its noise to douse.
Puzzled folk ran to hear from each house.
What could it be — this din?
Earthquake? Avalanche? Sin?
Wrong proved guesses when out came a mouse.

Aesop's Moral: "Don't make much ado about nothing."

The Contemporary Illustration

Milton E. called in Sally, his new secretary. This was her first day on the job, and she had had no indoctrination because Peggy, her predecessor, had left so abruptly. He had had to make do with girls from a temporary agency for nearly three weeks while he had rejected one incompetent after another that the employment office had sent for an interview.

He hoped Sally would fill the job. She was good looking, white, and had two years of college in addition to her training at secretary school. He wasn't prejudiced against blacks, he told himself, but Peggy had been too much. She had more domestic troubles than a soap opera heroine, and was forever out resolving a crisis for one member or another of her large family. Nor did she take her job seriously when she did come in.

"Why do we need these weekly activity reports, Mr. Edwards?" she would ask. "The men all complain about them, and all we do with them is to file them."

"Look, Peggy," he had explained more than once. "I have nine prima donnas reporting to me. I can't interface with each personally. These reports give me an overview on what they are doing."

"The men know that the reports are just checkups, Mr. Edwards, and they resent them for that reason. 'Police state mentality,' they say."

"Who says that?"

Peggy had refused to name anyone. This had been the final straw that had led him to discharge her. He had enjoyed overriding the objections to his action of the pettifogging manager of employee relations.

Now Sally stood before him, a trim girl of about twenty-one, he would judge. Of course he didn't know exactly. The employment office no longer asked job applicants' ages, claiming it was now illegal to do so, according to some ridiculous ruling from the government office of Equal Employment Opportunity.

"Oh, Sally, I want you to call the nine direct reports and tell them I need their deltas by noon before the meeting this afternoon."

"Excuse me, sir, but you will have to explain a couple of things — direct reports and deltas."

Milton smiled. "Of course, Sally, always stop me if I get technical. The nine direct reports are the nine people who report directly to me. You'll find their names and extension numbers on the wall chart beside your desk. And deltas are little symbols — filled-in triangles actually — which you will see on the chart. They signify completed projects."

Sally nodded. "That explains that, but I'm afraid you will have to explain some more about that chart. I can't make head or tail of it. What are those little circles beside some of the names? Some are filled in, some not."

Milton got up and went with her to her desk in the anteroom. On the wall was the chart, about six feet long and three feet high. It was a maze of deltas, circles, squares, and rectangles, dotted lines, solid lines, and dates. Each of the nine direct reports had a different color assigned to him.

Milton spent a happy half-hour explaining the chart to Sally. "It will be your job to keep this chart current," he told her, "so that I will be able to tell at a glance who's working on what, the status of the project, and so on."

She nodded thoughtfully. "How do I get the information to keep the chart up-to-date?"

"They report to you each day. Monday is delta day — today. You check everyone to see if they have completed any projects every Monday morning. That's, of course, for the projects for which they are primarily responsible. If it's half done, half fill in the triangle, etc. Tuesday is square day. That's to report on projects in which they play an important part but for which they do not have the prime responsibility. If it's completed, fill in the square completely, half-done, fill it half way, and so on. The arrow from the square points to the direct report who has the prime responsibility. Wednesday is rectangle day; rectangles symbolize projects for which the direct reports have only a minor role. The dotted lines point to the directs who have more important responsibility for it, but still not prime responsibility. The solid line points to the primes. Now Thursday is circle day — trouble — when people are going around in circles." Milton chuckled at his joke, and Sally managed a fleeting smile.

"What about Friday?" she asked.

"That's staff meeting day. We get organized for the coming week. Decide what to do about the trouble spots. And verify this chart. It comes off the wall, you see, and we take it to the conference room."

She nodded doubtfully. "It must have been there when I interviewed with you last Friday. I didn't see it then." She looked at it reflectively.

Milton bustled back into the office. "I know it looks formidable now, but you'll soon find your way around it. And you will find it as valuable as I do. I must say that the chart looks a little messy and complicated now because I haven't had a proper secretary in three weeks. You'll have to bring it up to date. But I'll help you with that. The first order of business, however, is to remind everyone about this afternoon's meeting. A planning session in the conference room."

He gave her instructions concerning it that dealt with flip charts, easels and admonitions not to be disturbed for any reason during the affair.

That afternoon, the planning meeting had progressed for nearly an hour when Sally entered the room.

"Sally, I told you I was not to be disturbed."

She said nothing as she handed him a note. It read, "President Blackwell says he wants to see you *at once*. He *ordered* me to interrupt."

Milton smiled. "That's all right, Sally. You did the right thing." He turned to nine other men in the room. "Well, gentlemen. Mr. Blackwell has something urgent he wishes to consult me about. Rather than waste your time while you wait for me, I suggest that we adjourn this affair until tomorrow morning, say nine-thirty?"

The nine quickly got up, almost as one man, and were out of the room on Milton's heels.

In the president's office, Blackwell barked without preamble: "What the hell is this about no interruptions?"

"My secretary is new, JB. She didn't understand."

"She seemed to have it very clear in her head that you had told her you didn't want to be interrupted for any reason."

"No, she had that wrong, JB I was just in a planning session."

"What, again! Hell, I'm glad I had her interrupt you." The president shifted in his chair. "I'm making a point of this because I keep wondering about your secretaries, Milton."

"Secretaries? What's the matter?"

"That last one you had, Peggy Macon. She's filed a complaint against us. Discrimination, the works. Read it and give me a draft of your rebuttal by five tonight." He tossed an official-looking document across the desk.

"But sir, I'll have to study this, have employee relations draw up a position paper. . ."

Blackwell slapped his hands on the desk. "I said I wanted the rebuttal from you, not employee relations. Employee relations is not involved in this. They told me they warned you when you fired Peggy." He held up his hand for silence as Milton tried to interrupt. "Milton, when I promoted you to office manager, I expected you to solve some of the administrative problems around here, not create new ones. Well, you've created one here that could be a dilly. Let's see how you propose to solve it."

"But. . ."

The president rose as he roared, "No more buts, no more 'position papers,' no more long-winded reports and planning meetings. I want action from you and you alone, and I want it by five o'clock. You haven't got much time. Get on with it."

Modern Precept for Promotion: "If you concentrate on the trivial, you'll overlook the important."

"Small causes may produce great results."

The Mouse and the Lion

Big Lion got caught in a net.
Miss Mouse was so small — and yet
She nibbled him free
As quick as could be,
After Lion spent hours of sweat.

Aesop's Moral: "Small causes may produce great results."

The Contemporary Illustration

Cramer W., now vice president of an auto company, looked like he had peaked out with that firm at the age of forty-three. He held a creditable job at that time with the company, but many in his age group were doing better than he in the organization. So, he accepted a vice presidency with a much smaller independent truck manufacturer where he filled the position brilliantly. Three years later, the auto management, seeking a top executive, scanned their outstanding alumni. He was tapped for the vice presidency at a total compensation that was ten times what he received when he had left the corporation.

You may get lost in the shuffle at a large company. Furthermore, a smaller or different organization may suit you better at certain stages in your career. Because of new and more varied experiences, perhaps Cramer, in three years with the truck manufacturer, reached a business maturity that would have taken much longer to achieve with the auto company.

Pete Jr.'s father was concerned at his son's job hopping. In twelve years he had held positions with five different small computer service firms. While he had advanced in title and salary with each move, Pete Sr. warned him that he had reached a point of diminishing benefits from his career strategy.

"I've reached the point of the big payoff," replied the son.

Indeed, he had. He soon landed a top management job with a major time-sharing firm, passing over several other men who had been with the new employer much longer than he and who were his age or older.

"If I had gone through the conventional chairs with the big parent of this outfit," he later explained to his father, "I probably wouldn't even have been able to get into their time-sharing subsidiary, and it's the newest and fastest growing part of the computer business. They needed someone with experience with smaller users of computers — the people who don't need or can't afford a computer of their own but who want to rent time on one. That's the kind of people I've been dealing with for a dozen years. All the old-timers in this outfit have experience primarily with big users of computers; they don't talk the same language as these little fellows, but I do."

So, you go to the smaller firm when you're blocked in promotions at the large, as in Cramer's case. Or you go small to get that kind of experience, as Pete did. I have more to say, incidentally, about job hopping in the fable of the "Milkmaid and her Pail," but here I can point out that the practice doesn't have the onus it once did. Yet if you run into an older man such as Pete Sr., watch out! He probably still nourishes all the shop-worn prejudices against someone who has been with more than three employers in twenty-five years.

There's a third reason often given for going small: To avoid or minimize bureaucracy. Watch out for this time-honored generality. Nit-pickers exist everywhere, although they seem to flourish better in the big than in the small environment.

A fourth reason for choosing the small environment involves creativity. A study of more than a hundred Michigan businessmen who ran their own small companies showed that, although the businessmen differed from each other in many ways, all shared one characteristic — creativity. Orvis F. Collins and David G. Moore, the Michigan State University authors of the survey, point out that the businessmen often deliberately placed themselves "in open positions because they would rather face the impersonal forces of the economy than cope with interpersonal relations that they find in the big, established organization."

As a product designer, Sam W. was attracted to a big diversified company because he reasoned that a broad product line would offer more opportunity for his talents. Yet in two years he had assignments that involved only three different products of the thousands that the company made. Furthermore, he never worked on a project from start to finish. He had a little piece of the action and rarely could recognize his own contributions in the end result.

He left for a little firm that made just one thing — wire coat hangers. Sam came up with all sorts of innovations for this seemingly simple product, ranging from a method for a retail store to imprint its name on it to a locking device to keep trousers from sliding off.

It's absurd for an organization to "systematize" for creativity as Sam's diversified company claimed that it did. Creativity cannot be reduced to a system. A climate of freedom may encourage creativity, but a "systematized" climate connotes restrictions, the enemy of creativity. Small firms seem to be able to achieve that free climate more readily than large, generally because of more informality, less red tape, fewer rules.

Other reasons — more varied work, usually more relaxed atmosphere and so on — also favor the small environment. In the fable of the "Hare and the Tortoise," we see that some disadvantages exist too, but at least consider the small environment in mapping your strategy for promotion.

Modern Precept for Promotion: "Bigness doesn't necessarily bring success."

"Bend not break."

The Oak and the Reeds

Giant Oak stood stiff in his conceit;
Did not notice slim Reeds at his feet.
When gales uprooted him,
Unharmed Reeds hooted him,
"You must break, we can just bend to meet."

Aesop's Moral: "Bend not break."

The Contemporary Illustration

A plumber presented a bill for fifty dollars to fix a pipe in a lawyer's home. "Why, I can't charge that much for my time in legal work," protested the lawyer.

"I know," said the plumber, "that's why I left law."

The anecdote illustrates a truth: You frequently reap richer rewards, tangible or otherwise, in your second career than in your first.

A common way to "bend" your strategy for promotion is to job hop. Yet, nearly all the examples we have studied thus far involve moves within the same career. Although you must "bend" still more to change from career to career, the results may prove even more satisfying than mere job hopping within your same field.

We have already met Trevor G. (in the fable of the "Crow and the Pitcher") who had a far more rewarding career running a mail order business than in clerking in a bookstore. And Sam W. found it more fun to design coat hangers than to be involved in the bits and pieces of design work for a large manufacturer of high-technology products (in the "Mouse and the Lion").

Yet career hopping presents hazards, too. Quentin N. returned with relief to mutual fund selling after briefly trying to run his father's business as a manufacturers' representative (in the "Goose with the Golden Eggs"). Nor did Bob I. (in the "Fox and the Grapes") find the academic world any more rewarding than business.

While career hopping is a relatively new phenomenon for substantial numbers of people now, exceptional individuals through the ages have followed many pursuits. Two hundred years ago, for example, Ben Franklin had careers as printer, journalist, politician, diplomat, inventor and postmaster. Still, the fact remains that our grandfathers, even our fathers, seldom changed careers. In this time of "future shock" we find that it's becoming much more common. One explanation is that the breakneck pace of technology makes knowledge obsolesce quicker. Engineers, particularly, find that what they learned in school is obsolete in about ten years. Just the fast pace of life makes people change careers — not only in engineering, but in marketing, production, employee relations, research, administration and their subdivisions.

Are there career dropouts — like school dropouts — who haven't got what it takes to make it? Undoubtedly some people change because of lack of aptitude or motivation. But I am focusing here on the person who has already spent time in one career, usually with at least modest success, who wants to change.

Friends considered Prentiss H. a successful radio executive. As is not uncommon in New York radio, he had moved from station to station. Job hopping had become a way of business life, until he finally rose to news director at one of the major stations in the area. He held this post for five years, a record for him, but he grew increasingly bored and dissatisfied.

"I found myself jaded," he recalls. "Nothing but crime, the weather and sports. At forty, I couldn't see doing this for the rest of my life."

Prentiss considered many courses. He looked into buying a small station in rural New England, but his wife didn't want to leave the metropolitan area. He investigated television news, but he couldn't find a comparable job. Reading the business opportunity classified ads, he answered one seeking a partner in a new publishing enterprise.

A reporter for a major publication that had recently discontinued sought a partner in a new monthly magazine he called *One Flight Up*. He proposed to put out a news and advertising periodical featuring the stores, shops and other enterprises one flight up in New York City. Prentiss put up some money and joined him as a partner working on both the reporting and business side. Prentiss' wife became intrigued too and joined the staff as the magazine flourished.

"We lost our boredom," recalls the former radio news director. "Both my wife and I encountered new people and challenges. We're both revitalized and have found a zest for work that I at least had almost forgotten."

Prentiss mentions the hazards too. "My income was only about half what it had been in radio for the first eighteen months. But now my wife and I are earning double what just I did in radio. She had worked off and on over the years, but now it's full time for her, and she loves it. The change in her is phenomenal."

At first Prentiss worried about wasting his education and experience gained in radio. "I'm surprised how much my radio background helps me here," he says. "Old radio friends give me leads on stories. My news background has been ideal for publication writing. And the radio advertising people have tipped me off on ad accounts who couldn't afford radio but who can handle our rates.

But you shouldn't change careers casually; if you do, the bend may become a break. It did for Bob when he went to the academic world, and it was a bad break for Quentin during his brief sojourn as a manufacturers' rep. You do have an investment in time, education, experience and simple tenure that you give up at least partly if you change. You should plan your career change. The elements of that plan should include the what, the why, the how and the when.

A lawyer-turned-plumber may be an unlikely switch, but stranger changes have occurred. Who would have expected that the technically educated Sam would find satisfaction with coat hangers that he never experienced with much more sophisticated products? The answer lies in the fact that he had complete responsibility for coat hangers and no discernible responsibility for the highly technical items.

Your new career should bear at least a tenuous connection with your former endeavors. Prentiss's news background carried over to the magazine. Sam and Trevor, too, found tie-ins between their old and new pursuits.

Significantly, Bob made a radical switch from business to the university world, and his lack of success in academia stemmed at least partially from his inability to use much of his business experience in his new career. While salesmanship was the common denominator for Quentin as a seller of mutual funds and manufactured products, that was not enough. The two types of products — intangible and tangible — didn't have enough in common.

Why change your career? Careers wear out, especially in technical areas. People need to change when they reach dead ends (as in Trevor's bookselling case) or when they run out of gas (as in the example of Prentiss). While there are many good reasons for changing your career, the best one is to gain greater satisfaction from the work at which you spend one-third of your time.

The most difficult challenge a new career puts to you is how to achieve it. The easiest way to reorient yourself is through your present employer. Big companies, particularly, even encourage career switches — making an accountant an employee relations man, transforming a person with an engineering background into manufacturing manager. While this is the easiest path, it's not the most common because only large companies have the diversity to permit or encourage it. The more common route lies with a new employer. Sam took that path. Yet a word of warning: You start almost on square one with the new employer, and you must prove yourself both as a person and as competent or promising in your new field.

Many people toying with a new career do so because they want to be their own boss. Prentiss and Trevor chose this route and succeeded. But more fail. Unless you enter one of the professions or the arts, the odds are against going alone with a new career. If your reasons for the career change hinge on self-employment, however, here are tips on how to plan for it and how to minimize the risks:

1. Go into a field where a need for your services exists. Both Trevor and Prentiss found such a niche, with little competition.

2. Go into a field that requires minimum financing. Inadequate financing causes most business failures. So, the less you need, the better.

3. Find an enterprise that needs few skilled employees. Inability to attract top people is the second most common cause of business failures. Prentiss' *One Flight Up* operated with just four employees — the partner, Prentiss and his wife and one secretary.

4. Operate with as little overhead as possible. While this relates to the financing and employee tips, still another factor makes this good sense. A high-overhead operation requires much administrative attention which the self-employed person can rarely afford.

5. Resign yourself to much hard work and long hours. The self-employed work harder, in general, than do those employed by others.

6. Plan to stay small. The person whose small enterprise grows large often finds himself facing the same dilemmas that led him to self-employment in the first place.

Sometimes the second career is thrust upon you without you consciously willing it to do so. The engineer may temporarily take on a special sales engineering job and do so well that he ends up permanently in marketing. Or the company lawyer may help out on one problem at the bargaining table and find himself in employee relations full time. Maybe these "accidental" shifts are good, but perhaps not. If you have doubts, it's well to have your return ticket already in hand — the right to return to your original career.

Timing is all-important in career change — both from the standpoint of your own age and from the circumstances around you. In the latter case, for example, it would not have made too much sense to shift to engineering or teaching in the early 1970s when the job prospects in each of those careers dimmed. Similarly, the lengthy educational requirements for medicine makes impractical the shift to that career in your middle or later years.

You should not change careers when it's too accidental or if the timing is poor, but there are other good reasons not to shift. For example: When the shift would mean too many changes — loss of income, moving to another area, radical adjustment in life styles; when the second career has too short a "half-life," as in the case of some branches of engineering; or when part-time experiments with the second career reveal unexpected drawbacks.

One of the ways to launch a second career with minimum risk is to pursue both your first and second careers at the same time. Trevor did that for a while, continuing both bookselling and his mail order business. Yet time and energy limit such double track operations for most of us to a relatively short period. Give it thought, however, as a test-the-water device when you launch a second career.

The second career is the ultimate weapon in your strategy for promotion — the bending that's just short of breaking. The second career offers you the opportunity to start fresh and avoid errors you made in your first. It's a second chance. Everyone has regrets and doubts, at least occasionally, about the wisdom of the first career choice. If you have the courage to launch a second course, you are doing something that may well lead to a more satisfying life.

Modern Precept for Promotion: "A bend — but not a break — in your career path may lead to a promotion."

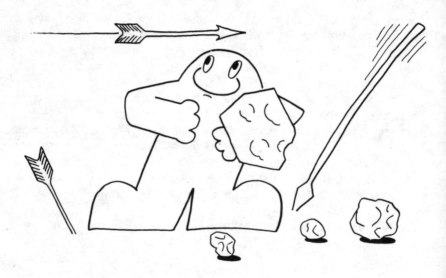

"Those who suffer most cry out the least."

The Ox and the Axletrees

The Ox sweated to pull the farm cart.
The axletrees had groaned from the start.
"Why do you so complain?"
Cried Ox as he did strain.
"All the worst damage falls on my heart."

Aesop's Moral: "Those who suffer most cry out the least."

The Contemporary Illustration

Vince surreptitiously looked at his watch — 11:30! He had been in here for nearly two hours while the old man raved with complaint after complaint. Now he was carrying on about the diodes they bought from an outside vendor.

"This is the worst crap yet they've given us," he was saying. "Make a note to give purchasing hell about this. We won't accept another shipment if they don't shape up."

"But Luke," protested his assistant. "We've got that one all cleaned up. They sent a replacement shipment already, along with profuse apologies."

"Well, why in the hell didn't you tell me?" The production manager slammed the offending diode into his wastebasket. "That's the trouble around here. I'm always the last to know. No communication."

"I wrote you a memo on that, at least a week ago. It must be in that pile on your back table."

"Christ, you and your memos. Why didn't you simply come in here and tell me?"

Vincent didn't explain that he had written a memo in an unsuccessful attempt to avoid a two-hour diatribe like this one had turned into. Instead, he said, "I wanted it all in writing in case purchasing gives us trouble. I thought you would have read the memo by this time."

Luke eyed him narrowly. "If I read all the crap that passes across my desk, I'd never get anything else done. That's your job, VD, to free me from the paper work."

Vince noted the use of his initials, a sure sign of the old man's annoyance and a ploy to get a rise out of him. In a careless moment, Vince had once confided to him that all during his boyhood neighbor kids had teased him about the initials. The use had long since ceased to bother him, but Luke apparently thought otherwise.

Vince dredged up a grin. "OK, LI," he said, his invariable rejoinder when the old man got into this mood. "If that's the case, I've got to get cracking." He started to leave, glad of an excuse, but the session wasn't over.

"Wait just one damn minute. You haven't told me the status on the new numerical control equipment. How much longer do we have to wait before the frigging debugging's finished?"

Vince raised his hands in mock despair. "That's all in a memo to you, also. I sent it two days ago. OK, OK. . ." He held up his hand as though stopping traffic when Luke started to protest. "I now know your views on memos. I'll report orally hereafter. The debugging will be finished by the end of this week. I checked things out earlier this morning, and it looks good."

The news didn't seem to cheer the production manager appreciably. "Alright, I can give Owings the word. He wants to see me this afternoon in one of his blasted meetings that will probably last forever — and on a Friday too, the sonofabitch."

Vincent gave a silent prayer of thanks to the company president for keeping the production manager lengthily occupied with something other than his assistant.

Until lunch time, Luke reminisced about his early days with the company stretching back forty-six years when he had joined at the age of sixteen. A few minutes before the production manager had to leave to keep a luncheon appointment, he asked, almost as an afterthought, "You were out on the factory floor this morning. Any other problems? And how are you coming on the modification for Western Industries' order?"

Vince got up gratefully. "No problems, at least as of 9:30 this morning. And the modification is in good shape. I'll have something for you first thing Monday. I'm going to check it out this weekend."

Luke just grunted as he put on his hat and coat.

Human nature being what it is, complaints are inevitable from the boss. Expect them; take them in your stride, as Vince did. Don't let them upset you unduly, but on the other hand don't take them too casually. Vince had learned to differentiate between the serious and the trivial. A common tendency is to give undue weight to everything the superior says. (For more on complaints in general, see the fable of "The Man That Pleased None.")

In his early association with the production manager, Vince had sat through a three-hour diatribe about excessive scrap. He had left the office ready for battle, but fortunately he had first checked the scrap figures. They showed a decline, not an increase. Puzzled, he had questioned the general foreman.

"Forget it," the veteran advised. "I can guess what happened. The old man was out here yesterday afternoon and happened to stop and watch a new kid we have on the drill presses. The youngster got so flustered with the big boss breathing down his neck that he botched a whole job. So the old man thinks the entire work force is going to pot on scrap."

On the other hand, recognize when your superior is serious. Vince knew that the debugging process on the new equipment rated top priority. He had been spending as much of his time as Luke didn't preempt, working with the crew sent in by the machine tool builder to expedite the job. So busy had he been with this that he would have to work over the weekend on the Western Industries modification. He knew what he wanted to do on that one, but he had not yet had time to verify the solution he had in mind.

Vince didn't have the trouble that relates to some management complaints. The boss may couch them so casually or gently that you miss their significance. Vince knew that practically all of Luke's complaints were exaggerated, so he adjusted accordingly.

But a word of warning: Are your own measuring scales always accurate? Do they indicate a complaint is unimportant because you want it to be so? Look at your own calibrations.

After trial and error, Vince had developed the following defenses against the production manager's gripes:

1. He diagnosed potential difficulties and potential trouble spots before they became serious or even difficult or troublesome. This involved constant alertness and being on top of his job. From experience, Vince learned where trouble usually developed first, and he kept an especially sharp eye on those areas.

2. He never lost his temper. He never let Luke see that he was annoyed or upset, even when he was.

3. He never blamed others. Vince learned that lesson during the episode of the new employee who became flustered when the old man had kibitzed next to him. He had told Luke that the scrap problem wasn't serious, just confined to a nervous youngster.

"Then fire the jerk," had been the production manager's solution. Vincent had not fired him, but transferred him to the night shift so that the old man would not see him.

4. He gave the full story. This really means guarding credibility. Vince recognized that he could forestall most of Luke's complaints simply by assuring him he need not worry — so much confidence had the old man in his assistant's honesty. Dishonesties of commission are relatively rare, of omission common.

In the case of the nervous employee, Vince erred in not telling everything — that the youngster grew anxious as almost any new-comer might if the big boss for half an hour stood a foot away from him. Instead, the assistant had simply said the employee was inexperienced and high strung, never spelling out the reasons for his anxiety. In Luke's shoot-from-the-hip style, the production manager never stopped to ask why.

5. Vince gave advance notice of trouble and triumphs. He had learned to follow an ancient axiom, "never surprise your boss, even pleasantly." He discovered the lesson about pleasant news the hard way. He had reported in triumph that the shop had exceeded a monthly production target.

"Yeah, I know," said Luke. "Owings told me an hour ago. And I felt like a Goddam fool, having to learn it from him."

"How did he find out?"

"Our buddies in accounting told him. Made it sound like they had produced every single friggin widget on their calculators."

Luke was justifiably annoyed, Vincent had to acknowledge, because he had been short-changed in getting full credit for his department's performance.

You should report unavoidable bad news as rapidly as possible for two reasons: To present the case the way you see it and to suggest what to do to remedy the situation. Disclosure by others may force you out completely.

6. Vince also watched for the true meanings behind the complaints. He understood some of the psychology that embittered Luke. As a "bull of the woods" type who had climbed from the factory floor to foreman, to general foreman and finally to production manager, he was a rarity in the company's management. With less formal schooling and polish than any other of his peers, he felt defensive. A man with drive, he knew now that he would never become company president, an ambition he had once held.

Vince made allowances for all this and even admired the old man for his common sense, down-to-earth practicality and intuitive knowledge of the business.

Late that afternoon, Vince was in his own office reminding himself of his boss's virtues, which he had to do after sessions like the one in the morning. A phone call interrupted him. President Owings wanted to see him. Vince surprised himself by not being surprised when he learned that Luke was taking early retirement and that he, Vince, had been Luke's choice and everyone else's to succeed in the job as production manager.

As soon as he could tactfully leave Owings, Vince rushed back to Luke's office.

"I fooled you this time, didn't I?" chortled his erstwhile boss. He held up his hand to stop Vince's words just as Vince had done to him that morning. "No pieties, boy. I've been thinking of doing this for a long time. I gave Owings my decision this afternoon. I know you'll do a great job here. And I know that you'll be glad to see the last of me. No, I want to say this. For the last year I've been a pain in the ass to everyone around me, but most of all to myself. I need to get out of here while I still have a little dignity left. You've let me keep some of that dignity, Vince. I appreciate that. For a kid, you're quite a guy."

"Every one of my thirty-eight years thanks you, sir. I hope I can still call on you for advice. I'll need it."

"Sure, I'm going to be a 'consultant,' whatever that is, for the three years until I reach sixty-five and can go on full retirement pay. They've done all right by me, financially; I have to give them that, although," he added with a grin, "the bastards could afford it."

Modern Precept for Promotion: "If you can field complaints well, you can win the game."

"Do not quarrel with nature."

The Peacock's Complaint

To the gods, Peacock would rant and rail,
"I want a voice like a nightingale."
The gods gave him this word:
"Be quiet, silly bird,
Swing your songs with your colorful tail."

Aesop's Moral: "Do not quarrel with nature."

The Contemporary Illustration

Ian B. chose Friday as the day he would resign, largely because he hoped that the inevitable furor which his action would cause would dissipate over the weekend.

"But why are you so set on doing this?" wailed the company president after Ian had told him his decision. "You've been with us twenty-five years. You just got a raise. I don't understand this going into business for yourself — and into plastics. You don't know the first thing about plastics!"

"I've been studying the field." Ian launched into an explanation of his decision — speaking smoothly because he had already rehearsed it several times in making it to his wife, father-in-law and friends.

"I've always had this yen to go into business for myself. I've been able to land an exclusive license on a new process for extruding plastics that looks promising. I realize that I know little about plastics, but I wanted an exclusive licensing arrangement in something with a future. Plastics are the materials of the future. Technically expert people tell me that this extruding process has great merit. A partner is going in with me who knows the technical side. He has some money to put into the venture, and so do I. I'll run the business end."

The president frowned. "Yes, but what about sales? You're an accountant."

Ian had an answer for that, too, because the objection had surfaced before. "If need be, we'll hire salesmen eventually, but for the time being my partner and I will handle that, too."

The president held out his hands. "But Ian, you've never sold a thing in your life."

Ian smiled, ready for this one, too. "Just because I haven't sold a product in a conventional way doesn't mean I can't sell. I sell you every quarter on the best way to present the company figures. I sell all the department heads on the need to submit new reports, like that one we started last month on scrappage."

"You didn't sell that one. I did. And I don't know if it's sold yet. I had another gripe about it yesterday."

Ian waved the disclaimer aside. "Well, I sold you on the need for the scrap report and you picked up the ball."

Ian left the session with the president, exasperated but more determined than ever to do what he planned. Almost everybody objected to his decision — wife, father-in-law, the president, even some of his friends. But that was the trouble when you tried anything new. Everybody pictured good solid Ian as set for life in this job as chief accountant for a company that he had been with since graduating from college.

He had to get out of this rut, Ian told himself. He felt trapped.

Ian snapped the pencil he had been holding in two.

He was bored with the sameness of this job. While he had indeed just won a raise, his income was nothing sensational. He and Madge were having trouble financing their five children's college educations. The plastics business offered him a chance to make it really big, build an estate, maybe even retire at sixty as his father-in-law had, never to have to work again.

Ian and his partner went ahead with their plans, but in six months they had to face defeat. The extruding equipment they had ordered didn't work out as expected. Electricity rates, a major part of their costs, went up sharply and threw their cost plans seriously awry. They could have perhaps jumped both those hurdles, but not the third. As the nay-sayers had predicted, sales proved the worst problem. Ian tried to handle that aspect of the business, but without success. They hired a salesman, and that move compounded their budgetary difficulties. Furthermore, he didn't produce.

Ian and his partner tried to raise more money, but without success.

Why do otherwise intelligent people make errors in their career planning that are obvious to almost everyone but themselves? Why do they persist, even for six months, in their folly? Many reasons account for such errors, but these four stand out:

1. *Because of shock and / or panic.* This figured to some degree in precipitating Ian into his ill-fated plastics venture. In two years' time he would have three children in college all at once. The prospect so dominated his thoughts that he couldn't think straight on other matters. At the moment, he had trouble enough just financing one daughter's edu-

cation. He could not see how he could handle two, let alone three, without a drastic increase in income; which he had hoped plastics would provide.

2. *Because of outside pressures.* The challenge of education was one outside pressure, but other money matters forced themselves upon him. He and Madge lived well, because, he kept telling himself, Madge had been used to an exalted standard of living before they were married and expected it to continue. He had to admit that he liked it himself. In the style of life they had developed for themselves. Ian and Madge moved in circles where many of the men owned their own businesses or held high positions in well-known companies. Ian envied them, and Madge made pointed comments now and then about his prosaic title, chief accountant.

3. *Because of inner pressure.* Ian suffered from middle-aged syndrome. He shuddered at the thought of continuing on for eighteen more years until retirement doing the same old thing. He saw little chance of further advancement. He had more than his share of vanity which contributed to his disastrous decision.

4. *Because of poor self-knowledge.* Despite his quarter century of working and his near-half century of living, Ian knew little of himself when he moved to plastics. He had been "on the conventional middle-class track" all his life, as he admitted later in post-morteming his new experiences. He had attended public high school in Cleveland, won his accounting degree at Ohio State, then moved directly to the firm that employed him uninterruptedly for twenty-five years. He lacked even the leaven of military experience because of a heart murmur. He and Madge had always been able to live beyond his income because Madge's father continued to give her an allowance after marriage.

"I was never forced to think deeply about myself, my abilities and my goals in life." Ian could acknowledge later.

I have commented before about knowing yourself, especially in the fables of the "Fox and the Grapes" and in "Horse and Man." Now, let's go a step further. Actually, knowing yourself is taking stock of yourself as a person. The secret of good stock-taking lies in becoming thoroughly aware of what things matter to you a great deal and what things don't.

From this knowledge you become aware of your inner needs or drives. Regardless of what they are, they determine the kind of person you are. Three exercises can help you take stock and get important knowledge of yourself.

1. Write out at least ten answers to the question, Who am I? Obviously, you might be a business man or engineer. But think further. I am

a husband and father. I'm a dreamer rather than a doer. Those are just samples. Get started but don't stick to these too much. Let your thoughts range and include both good or bad traits. At this point, don't start reading meaning into the answers. In this part of the exercise, you just gather information.

2. The next task is to list things you have done well — specific tasks that have brought you praise or given you personal satisfaction. These can be quite simple, even unimportant. But you should put them down if you remember them with pleasure. Think back; don't limit yourself to recent events.

The second part of this exercise is to prepare a list of what you have had to do, for whatever reason, but which you didn't enjoy and didn't do particularly well. They can relate to your present job, home, education, vacations. Again, these events need not have been earth-shaking — just what you remember readily. The idea is to learn the type of activities that has given you the least sense of personal satisfaction and accomplishment.

3. With a completely free choice and none of the usual limiting factors, what would you most like to do? Think hard about this. These can be of either long or short duration, important or unimportant, vocational or avocational, and even things you have never done but would like to do.

With the three exercises finished, you're now ready to review what you have listed. Do it carefully. Does a pattern emerge? And no cheating! Be objective. Your future may depend on your honesty.

When you have completed the review, share it with at least one other person — but preferably two. Good candidates might be people interested in such a self-survey for themselves. Compare notes with these people. Note how unique you are, how different from the others who go through the exercise. Don't discuss the findings from the standpoint of right or wrong. Look at them descriptively.

Once the new perceptions of yourself have become settled and you can look at them objectively, begin to use the new insights to make decisions which affect your career. With new perspectives, career planning should be much simpler and your goals in better focus.

Ian went through the exercises after the plastics fiasco. He discussed the findings with his wife and with his partner, who had actually introduced him to the practice because he had found himself as up in the air as Ian.

These patterns did emerge for the accountant: He did need a change, although not as drastic a one as he had tried, because he had grown stale and lacklustre. He had always wanted to go into business for himself and still did. He yearned for more variety in his work and his life than he had been experiencing. His worries about money, while real, were not as serious as he had imagined. His children could contribute more to their own educational expense, and he and Madge could reduce their scale of living.

Many people, like Ian, need a career change from time to time, as already noted in the fable of "Horse and Man." If you know yourself well, six choices, basically, face you when you feel restless in your job, dissatisfied but not forced into immediate action.

1. You can do nothing. Don't laugh. Your situation may be only temporary. Unforeseen developments may occur to change the conditions that cause your difficulty. If that's your case, the biggest advantage in having done nothing is that no risks, financial or otherwise, were undertaken.

On the other side of the coin, the situation may deteriorate. Among the disadvantages of doing nothing is that the situation may grow even more desperate for you. Your performance could worsen, even to the point of discharge.

So, the frequency or the duration (or both) of the troublesome situation is the main criterion to apply when considering the "do nothing" option.

2. Quit and take another job fast. The advantages lie in the possibility of more money and a quick end to the troubles on the other job. And a psychological lift usually results from making a fresh start.

Yet a quick move poses disadvantages, as Ian learned at his cost. Fast action usually means inadequate investigation of all other possible courses of action and of the job you have so quickly taken. That proved Ian's undoing in the plastics venture. His new work proved even less tenable than his old.

3. Withdraw. Leave the business-industrial-management environment and try Indian basket weaving or whatever else you fancy.

Recently, an increasing number of able and intelligent businessmen have opted for this course. But note that in nearly all successful examples of withdrawal, the individual had something to which he could withdraw — a hobby that becomes all engrossing, an artistic bent that he has followed avocationally in the past, an interest that he has pursued for years.

Ian felt no compulsion to withdraw. He had never been artistic, nor did he pursue any hobby that promised to support him.

4. Arrange a transfer within the company. This is almost impossible in a small company, difficult in a medium-sized firm, and practical to a significant extent only in a large firm.

Ian had worked for a small outfit, so the transfer route had been closed. But if it can be arranged, there's much to recommend this course.

5. Land an offer. Carefully plan and execute a campaign that leads to an offer of a new job somewhere else.

The advantages lie in financial gain, the end of present difficulties and the psychological lift.

The disadvantages of this course lie mainly in the time it takes and the possibility that it may mean geographical and other changes which you may not wish to accept. Ian didn't even consider this possibility, so enamored was he with the plastics business.

6. Try to improve the situation. Just thinking about the problem and trying to analyze its causes may result in some improvement. The obvious advantage, if you can improve the situation, is to avoid loss of the tangible assets that accompany the job and the pleasure derived from regaining satisfaction in the work.

The biggest disadvantage: The situation may simply defy improvement. That was the case for Ian because the dissatisfaction lay more with him than with the job itself.

No one of these courses is best for all situations. Consider carefully each option. On the second time around, Ian did at last give careful thought to his future. He decided to start his own business as a certified public accountant. It meant a change, but not as dramatic a career shift as the move to plastics. It met his long-felt desire to go into business for himself. This time, his wife and father-in-law enthusiastically supported him, the latter even helping to finance him at the start and giving him business leads.

Modern Precept for Promotion: "Use the gifts you have because you'll never be able to use those you lack."

"Nobody believes a liar, even
when he tells the truth."

The Shepherd and the Wolf

A Shepherd Boy, not thinking much,
Gave false alarms of "Wolf!" and such,
Till none came to his yelp
Of "Help, help, help, help,"
When a real wolf put him in Dutch.

Aesop's Moral: "Nobody believes a liar, even when he tells the truth."

The Contemporary Illustration

Remember Jay D., the product promoter who came a cropper in the "Fox and the Grapes" fable? He started on the new product-publicity job, presumed to be honest until proved a liar. It soon became obvious that he had exaggerated his expertise about mailing lists. That alone didn't do him in, but he damaged his credibility still more by another kind of exaggeration that's all too common. He would tell vendors that he needed something by "five tonight" when he actually didn't need it until next week. He would ask his secretary for ten copies but he needed only three. When trying to get colleagues to cooperate with him, he would shamelessly name-drop, implying that the boss personally had a hand in the project although his connection really was remote.

All these slips were bad but not fatal.

He signed a death warrant for his credibility — and job — by exaggerated charges about poor planning for a trade show and ridiculous claims about the uses of direct mail. His boss never believed anything he said thereafter.

Persistent exaggeration probably ruins more promotional opportunities than any other credibility gaffe. Why do some people exaggerate so?

One reason: Because overstatement is an affliction of this age. Politicians compare a relatively blameless opponent to Adolf Hitler. Newspaper headlines shout of "the worst disaster" in history. Advertisements scream of "the greatest product advancement" since sliced bread.

Some people exaggerate because "there's no harm in it — everybody does it." Yet there is harm in it for the job-holder — because habitual exaggeration makes difficult or even impossible good decisions and recommendations for action if the facts that influence the decisions or recommendations are overblown.

Another common reason for exaggeration is to seek credit or avoid blame. Jay committed these sins, too. The cumulative result was his departure.

The outright lie in the "cry wolf" situation proves relatively rare in the contemporary promotional situation, but the half-truth crops up frequently.

Vic W. had a job offer that meant a promotion of sorts to advertising manager with a competitor. He didn't really want to move to the new employer who was smaller and less progressive, but a promotional opportunity existed within his own organization. So, he mentioned the competitive proposal to his boss, implying that he would take it, unless of course the boss could give him the better job in his own organization. The boss told Vic he had better take the competitor's offer.

Poor Vic! He didn't want to move at all, but he had maneuvered himself into a position where he had to go to the other company or look like a fool. As it turned out, he became a fool for moving because the new employer merged into another firm and he found himself without a job a year later. While nobody wants to look like a fool, that's not as bad as being one.

The boss had let Vic go because he already harbored suspicion about the man's veracity. Doubts had arisen about certain claims on the expense account, but the boss had passed them without challenge. Vic had excused his frequent absences with colorful explanations. His daughter had been bitten by a neighbor's dog so she had to be rushed to the hospital; court appearances and other complications stemming from the dog-bite episode cropped up for several months thereafter. Another string of absences allegedly arose from a fire in his home. Although both the dog bite and the fire had occurred, their ramifications were embellished by the imagination of an ad man.

Yet, the boss never directly challenged any of this and therefore also committed a half-truth by not openly expressing his skepticism. Before his final half-truth to the boss, Vic already lived in a fool's paradise, thinking he could get away with making his life sound like a television soap opera.

The "cry wolf" syndrome crops up frequently in absenteeism. Millie R. missed out on a promotion to an executive secretary. Despite somewhat excessive absences, her superiors excused her both because she was efficient when she did appear and because of a whiplash back suffered during an auto accident. Millie used this to great effect in winning an insurance claim, too. However it no longer seriously bothered her. When she didn't become executive secretary, she of course asked for an explanation.

"That whiplash back," her superior said sadly. "The vice president said he just couldn't afford to have someone working for him who might be forced to be out frequently."

Her assurances that her back was "getting better" didn't prove persuasive in the light of her continued absences.

Jim R., the conglomerate promoter in the "Hare and Tortoise" fable, who went to prison for stock fraud, tried a number of business activities after he had served his sentence. Although he was scrupulously honest, nobody thought he could be. He finally found his level as a used car salesman.

"Everybody thinks all used car people are crooked," he says bitterly, "so the customers treat me with the same suspicion they give to all of us in this trade."

The chronic needler and practical joker also runs the risk of falling into the "cry wolf" trap. While his fall may not be as dramatic as Jim's, it may ultimately be as far, as in the case of Joe L.

He seldom could risk the not-so-subtle barb thrown into colleagues and even superiors, although the latter usually got the treatment when their backs were turned. His impressive talent for mimicry amused everyone but the victim.

Joe's crowning achievement was an anonymous letter circulated at a headquarters meeting concerning employee relations, urging white-collar employees to join a union and naming two well-known conservatives among their ranks as the leaders of the drive. Predictably, the conservatives were incensed, leading to a storm that at first delighted and then belatedly alarmed Joe. He denied authorship of the letter, although most people suspected him because of his well-known personality traits. While no one could ever pin the escapade on him, his boss remained convinced of his guilt. A chastened Joe cut down on his needling and never again wrote elaborate spoofs — but it was too late. He didn't get a promotion for which he had been considered. For a year he received the cold-shoulder treatment until he got the message and left the company.

Shakespeare's observation that "the evil that men do lives after them, the good is oft interred with their bones" proved too true in his case. His reputation as a joker preceded him, and he had to remain content with low-level jobs for the rest of his working life.

Modern Precept for Promotion: "Credibility is everything in winning advancement."

"Use your reason."

The Sick Lion and the Ass

A Lion cried from his redoubt,
"Come in, give me relief from gout."
The animals en masse
Advised aid, save smart Ass:
"I'll go in if others come out."

Aesop's Moral: "Use your reason."

The Contemporary Illustration

Sometimes the best promotion is the one you didn't get. In many fables thus far, we have seen cases where promotions went awry. Examples:

● When Quentin N. took over his "retired" father's business — briefly (in the "Goose with the Golden Eggs").

● When Louis M. took a poor job risk in Texas (in the "Geese and the Cranes").

● When George E. came a cropper because he moved to a new company without getting all the facts (in the "Blind Men and the Elephant").

● When the job-hopping Carol T. kept going after the right teaching jobs, but for the wrong reason of impatience (in the "Hare and the Tortoise").

Promotions can go wrong, too, when the candidate fools himself or is tricked by others. In these cases, mutual deception almost invariably proves a factor in the problem. The candidate wants the promotion too badly, and the employer wants him too urgently.

Getting promoted usually means a new job, even if the employer remains the same. That, in turn, sets up new conditions and relationships, again even if the employer remains the same. To avoid pitfalls that can turn an apparent promotion into a demotion, analyze the opportunity from the standpoint of yourself, of the new job, of the new boss and new employer (if any), and of new relationships with people.

● *Analyze yourself.* The first question you should ask yourself is whether you even want a promotion. But doesn't everybody? By no means.

As we have already seen, Jack M. (in the "Fox and the Grapes"), wisely refused the first promotion offered because it didn't suit his talents. Jack did something we all should do — studied himself and came up with a reasonably objective analysis. Note that I say "reasonably objective." Very few of us can be fully objective, but we should try to approach that ideal. Here's one way:

Learn what your bosses have said about your work. Check old performance appraisals, career discussions, accomplishment reports, awards.

Learn what others think you do well. If this doesn't come out from written reports of your bosses, go ask some reasonably objective people for their opinions, but tell them why you ask.

Decide what kinds of assignments have given you trouble or made you uncomfortable. You are your best source for information here. Think about your job troubles in the past. Come on now — be honest.

Decide the things that you have enjoyed most on or off the job. It's normal psychology to enjoy that which we do well. This doesn't mean that it is the thing we find easiest to do. A good job always has challenge. Sift through your list and sort out the winners. If it's necessary to rank the best, give one check mark for things you enjoyed the most, another check mark for things that were most successful, and still another for things you would like to do more of. The item or items with the most check marks are your strengths.

Does the preferred promotion line up with your strengths, at least approximately? If not, don't accept. If it does, that starts you toward a decision, but you aren't quite ready for it yet.

• *Analyze the new job itself*. Even if you decide that the promotion would provide a job that matches your skills well, you should decide if the new position has merit. You must find answers to these questions:

Why is the job open? What are you expected to accomplish in the first six months? The first ten years? Are there any unique problems that stand in the way of getting the job done?

Ben K., the banker in the "Fox and the Crow," did not or refused to realize that he was being lured into the vice presidency of another bank on the strength of his father's reputation in banking. He should have realized, if he had thought deeply, that the job was a newly created one. Why? What was he to accomplish? What had he to offer? He never dug below the surface to answer these questions.

To get answers in depth, you need honesty, investigative skill, patience and energy. If the promotion is to a higher rank within your own organization, you can get the information almost by osmosis, so familiar should you be with the situation. But if the job is outside your organization, especially a completely different employer, you need detective work. Friends and friends of friends are good sources. But the best source is your prospective new employer or boss; ask him. If you get satisfactory answers, you come closer to a decision, but hold off for still more answers in the next category.

• *Analyze the new boss and/or employer*. A crucial jigsaw piece that must be fitted in to estimate how you will fare with your promotion is your appraisal of your new boss and/or employer. Of course, you may not have a new boss or employer as a result of the promotion. Perhaps your present boss has created a new position for you. Then you already have this piece neatly in place. But usually at least a new manager would be in the offing.

Is he a hard driver? A team builder? Does he have any unique expectations of people who work for him? What method does he use most frequently for communication? How does he measure performance?

Your source here has to be largely your own perceptions because the man-manager relationship is so personal that what will work between one pair of people will prove an anathema to another. Yet, you at least can learn how the new boss has paired with others. If he has a reputation for difficulty, weigh the reason for such troubles. For example, the last straw for Lou in the abortive stint with the Texas-based jewelry firm was that he couldn't get along with the company's president. Their chemistry didn't mix. Lou should have suspected this because he was the fourth man to hold the job in three years.

If you go to a new business, ask questions such as these: What is the current growth pattern in the industry and what is the projected growth? Who are the key competitors and what's their competitive edge, if any?

If you go to a new employer still in your same business, you can answer the above questions of course, but you need additional information about the employer himself. For example, what is his share of the served market? Of the total market? Where does the company stand in technology relative to the competition? What does the current and projected growth curve look like? What is the sales volume, net income, number of employees, for the last few years? Are there remote plant locations? Will you be expected to travel?

You can pick up information of this sort from the company's annual report, from newspaper and magazine articles and from the prospective employer himself. Take care, however, to gather some of this data before you ever interview for a job promotion with a new employer.

When you have done all this, you have just one step more before you decide if you will take the promotion.

• *Analyze new relationships with people*. Even if you consider a promotion within your present component, remember that you will experience subtly different relationships with the very people that you now count as friends and supporters.

Jack, who eventually refused the first promotion offered as manager of accounts receivable, did so for several reasons. One was his opinion that the people he would be supervising would not readily accept him as their manager. He had been working with them and had achieved good camaraderie. He knew the old relationship would end if he became their manager, but he doubted that a good man-manager arrangement could easily or quickly develop. He foresaw resentment, a bad basis on which a manager must start.

Thus, if you want promotion and also want to avoid pitfalls, you prepare yourself for promotion — you analyze yourself and your objectives and you develop your contacts. This last is a subject in itself, touched on in "Hercules and the Wagoner," the "Bundle of Sticks," the "Ungrateful Wolf" and the "Hart and the Vine."

Modern Precept for Promotion: "The best promotions don't just happen; you use intelligence to make them happen."

"We may meet our match."

The Snake and the File

A hungry Snake mistook for food
A file that lay rusty and crude.
Said the File, "Don't mistake.
I'm accustomed to take.
To give is never in my mood."

Aesop's Moral: "We may meet our match."

The Contemporary Illustration

Remember the boy who was always the first to turn the whole gang against the new kid on the block? As an adult, he can be heard saying, "I understand Dave didn't make his third-quarter quotas — even after cooking the figures."

Greg Z., who made that snide remark, was fiercely competitive type who had repeatedly triumphed over the years playing "elimination" games.

Elimination games occur usually in highly bureaucratic organizations where office politics determine promotions more than competence. But Greg erred disastrously in targeting Dave G. for elimination. As a veteran salesman, Dave had survived for more than two decades because he knew even more tricks than Greg. Furthermore, he had been awaiting a chance to score against Greg whom he sensed was after his lucrative territory.

When Dave heard of Greg's knife-in-the-back tactics, he pretended indignation although he was secretly delighted. He saw a way to turn the strategy around because Greg's gossip was not quite accurate and because Greg had a vulnerable point himself. True, Dave had missed the quarterly quotas, but he had not been so stupid as to fudge figures upward to make the target. He had fudged them *downward* — in a way almost to defy detection. He would gamble that Greg was just guessing. Dave had simply held out a report on one good sale so that it would appear in the following quarter and make almost certain his reaching or exceeding the next period's target. If he had logged the sale in the third quarter, he still would not quite have made it, and he well knew that a miss by $1,000 was as bad as $10,000 as far as the sales manager was concerned. When he guessed that Greg's gossip had had time to reach the sales manager, he visited the boss.

"I think we should talk to Greg," he said, shaking his head sadly. "The guy gossips like a malicious old woman, making all kinds of wild statements about every guy on the sales force. Just yesterday I had to tell him that if he made one more snide remark about Gladys I'd bust him one."

"What's he saying about Gladys?" asked the sales manager uneasily as he got up to close the office door so that the lady in question, his secretary, couldn't hear.

"Dirty stuff. Working his imagination hard over the time she came to our Chicago sales meeting."

"Dave, you know Gladys came because we needed a secretary at that meeting. There's nothing hanky panky between Gladys and me."

Dave raised his hand like a policeman stopping traffic. "I know, and that's why I got so mad. Frankly, Greg shouldn't drink. He can't handle the sauce and starts talking like this after the second martini."

"Drinking, eh? I've wondered about him."

"Yeah, I've been noticing it, but hated to say anything. He had to be put to bed in Chicago."

This last was a shrewd thrust because Greg and two others had become drunk after the meeting in a well-publicized episode that the sales manager had dismissed at the time as a boys-will-be-boys incident.

The manager slapped his hand on the desk. "I'm going to have a talk with Greg."

Dave repeated his traffic cop gesture. "But not about Gladys. That might make you look like you have a guilty conscience. Let me take care of him about Gladys."

The sales manager hesitated. "Yeah, I guess you're right, but I'm going to blast him for this knife-in-the-back stuff he's been doing with my guys. I won't stand for it, and he's going to know it."

Dave kept a grave expression on his face until back in his office when he smiled broadly. His confidence was justified. Greg transferred to another division one month later.

Individuals get involved in games like these because advancements don't result from any particular merit evident to the participants. Instead, they see politics and gamesmanship as the twin routes to success. Therefore, many ambitious people travel those roads. Result? A polluted organizational environment with ineffective and inefficient operations. No wonder that some organizations — even generally successful ones — fumble as much as they do!

Not only do these games lead to major problems, they also prevent satisfactory solutions. The games foster an interchange based on ambiguity and deception. This stifles creativity, contaminates problem-solving efforts, hampers decision making and distorts communication.

Individual creativity is directed more at playing the games than trying to deal with the underlying problems. Gamesmanship leads to patchwork solutions to problems or, even worse, a buried problem. The decision-making atmosphere demands safe as opposed to effective action. Communication gets filtered to the point of becoming false or innocuous or both.

Behind gamesmanship lies fear — of being fired, demoted or overlooked. Dave and Greg had both lived in such fear for so long that they had developed their elaborate and ruthless games almost without realizing the effects on themselves and their organization.

Gamesmanship had cheapened their personalities and characters and had weakened the organization. Their manager should have realized this, but he had played — and continued to play — the games himself. Without a games-free manager, there's almost no hope of a games-free organizational environment.

If you find yourself in an environment where games are played and if you can't do much about it personally, you have just one course — leave. Belle Y. perhaps did a favor for Sally T., the gentle science teacher whom the dragon secretary maneuvered out of a job in the fable of the "Dog in the Manger." Gamesmanship was rampant at that school, and Sally was well out of the situation.

Of course, games-free environments do exist. Even here, people can meet their match, but the outcome is usually less disastrous for the loser. Harvey B. met his match in Connie S., the furniture buyer in the fable of the "Hare and the Tortoise," but nothing disastrous happened to Harvey. He continued as the assistant, swallowed his disappointment and masked his hurt pride behind his role of the dilettante. Connie had won her promotion on merit; even Harvey admitted that, although grudgingly.

Sometimes a person refuses to compete, but wishes to remain with the organization. In a gamesmanship environment, that person is doomed to a dim life in the working world, as Sally would have been had she stayed.

In an atmosphere free from gamesmanship, the non-competitor has a somewhat better prospect. Isabel A. apparently didn't want to compete. As an assistant copy editor for a business magazine, she liked her work and had done it competently for nearly ten years. When the copy editor retired, the managing editor called her in.

"Isabel," he said after the preliminary pleasantries, "how would you like to be the chief copy editor?"

"Oh, I don't know about that."

"It would be a promotion and more money."

"Yes, but the responsibility! I don't know. I'd have to think about it."

Isabel came in again the next day. After beating about the bush with explanations that her husband didn't want her to work overtime, that a man would do better in the occasional wrangles with reporters over stories and that she didn't want the added responsibility, she turned the promotion down.

In essence, she had met her match — not in another person, but in herself. Rightly or wrongly, Isabel had decided that the higher position didn't suit her. Perhaps she had taken Peter's principle to heart and feared that she would have moved from a level of competency to one of incompetency as chief copy editor.

Sometime later after the managing editor had filled the position with someone else who had worked out well, he fell to reminiscing about Isabel with his superior.

"I was annoyed, you know, when Isabel turned me down. But I think now that she was right. She continues to do a good job, and seems happy. In her, we still have a good assistant copy editor. If I had promoted her, I suspect now that I would have lost a good gal and gained a poor one."

Modern Precept for Promotion: "You may have gone as far as you can go."

"A crust of bread in peace is better
than a feast in fear."

The Town Mouse and the Country Mouse

Country Mouse joined Town Mouse's meal —
As rich a sup as you could deal.
But a cat pouncing quick
Made the Country Mouse sick,
And she had to flee home to heal.

Aesop's Moral: "A crust of bread in peace is better than a feast in fear."

The Contemporary Illustration

Ken R. grew impatient with his progress in the public relations department of a large manufacturer. He joined a major public relations agency and moved ahead fairly rapidly — but still not fast enough. He next formed his own PR firm.

At first he prospered because he had taken two accounts with him. But one dropped him in six months for a rival. New accounts proved hard to come by, but he finally landed two to make up for the loss of one. One was a slow payer, and the other became a no-payer when it declared bankruptcy. Ken's young firm soon followed into dissolution.

Now Ken tried to return to the agency field, but prospective employers knew he had pirated accounts before and shied away from hiring him. He used the one good account that he still had as a lure. When a smaller agency took the bait, Ken thought he had landed his fish until the bait itself vanished. The account he offered decided it had had enough of Ken and took its business elsewhere. Ken finally returned to the public relations department of another major manufacturer. His adventure into the richer life of agency PR had cost him four years, an ulcer, and a divorce. PR associates that had stayed with his first employer were far ahead of him now in job levels and income.

Of course, the yearning for the richer life can have a happier ending. Albert J., the solid citizen whom we left picking up the pieces of a shattered conglomerate in the fable of the "Hare and the Tortoise," eventually succeeded in reassembling a successful business. In the process, he became a wealthier man. But the two showed radically different approaches. Ken wanted the richer life first — and fast — and chose a means of getting it second. Albert reluctantly took on the reassembling job and slowly became rich as a by-product.

The point is not that you should never take risks, but that you should avoid risks that are perilous because of personal or other deficiencies. Ben K. took a foolish chance in becoming a vice president at a scandal-tainted bank (in the "Fox and the Crow" fable). Ken lacked the inclination to work long hours and the ability to manage other people successfully; traits that are essential for an effective entrepreneur.

Olivia A. learned to feast, but not in fear. As a statistical analyst in media research for a broadcasting firm, she was intelligent and bored; competent but performing a job with her left hand only; self-assured but tense in a job beneath her abilities. In short, she was underemployed. She eventually bestirred herself enough to find a much better job in media research with a large advertising agency where she was employed at her proper level for the first time in years.

Not so incidentally, moving to an employer in trouble may not be turning to a feast-in-fear situation but to a feast-in-excitement environment that some people find exhilarating. Albert experienced that reaction with his scaled-down conglomerate.

Olivia went to an ad agency with no media research worthy of the name; hence the agency was in trouble and knew it. She won a salary 50 per cent higher than that at the broadcasting company because the agency was willing to pay to get itself out of trouble. The lesson of Olivia: If you wish to sample the much richer life, consider an employer in trouble or at least one who thinks he's in trouble.

He's willing to buy his way out of his difficulties. Still more important, he's amenable to change — even eager for it. At the agency, Olivia easily got permission to try statistical techniques which the broadcaster had never permitted because that successful firm saw no reason to experiment when its established ways had proved themselves. While Olivia's new environment was at first less stable than her former one, she soon stabilized it by revitalizing the agency's media research. Albert, too, succeeded in stabilizing the mini-conglomerate.

However, what should you do if you wonder if you can create stability out of chaos? If in doubt, move only with caution. If apprehensive about the prospect, you should probably stay where you are. If you're genuinely worried, don't move under any circumstances. To master the unstable environment, you need self-assurance above everything else, an attribute which both Albert and Olivia possessed in ample measure.

It's all very well to talk about moving to an unstable situation with your eyes open, but what happens if you find you have unwittingly landed in such a situation? Ken found himself in that predicament, and he should have known better. He had enough experience in public relations to have realized the risks involved in forming a new, small agency. Yet he couldn't or didn't choose to see the chances he was taking.

If you insist on keeping your eyes shut, there's not much to be done to help you. But, there are signs that indicate instability if you want to look for them. A few among many:

- *The swinging door*. Predecessors in the job that interests you have come and gone with suspicious regularity. Why? If the interviewer explains this as happenstance or if he ascribes too varied shortcomings to the previous incumbents, look out. In Olivia's case, the interviewer frankly admitted that the agency had budgeted too little for the media research operation in the past and had received only what it paid for. Now it was prepared to pay for top quality. Although she faced a possible swinging door herself, she accepted the explanation for why it had formerly revolved so much.

- *A vague job description*. This almost invariably signals trouble. The employer doesn't know what he wants. If you can't force him to become specific, don't take the promotion offer because the employer shows himself as indefinite and/or vacillating. If instability doesn't turn up immediately, it will eventually.

- *A negative job description*. The employer knows what he doesn't want, but is much less certain about what he requires. This often leads to the swinging door, and it usually comes after the employer has tried the vague job description on previous candidates.

- *The hard, hard sell*. When the prospective employer acts like a used car salesman, take care. No job ever exists that has no drawbacks, but your suspicions should rise if he mentions none. You should refuse the offer if he denies any drawbacks exist.

- *Cautions from third parties*. Check the opinions about the prospective job environment from disinterested third parties if you can find them. One negative report doesn't necessarily queer the whole deal, but two should give you pause, and the third should constitute clear evidence that the proposal is not for you.

To get objective third-party views may not be easy. The best way is to canvass friends and acquaintances. While they may know nothing about the situation, they often can introduce you to someone who does. If an executive recruiter approaches you, don't rely too much on him for objectivity. He has a service to sell. You can count on state employment agencies to be a little, but not much, more forthright. They too sell a service. Among agencies, the most disinterested are the not-for-profit, privately sponsored groups that help with placement, particularly for older or minority-member applicants. Forty Plus of Southern California is an example. It's one of the largest organizations in the United States doing this work. As a voluntary, self-help group, it provides the mechanism whereby members, all over forty years of age and candidates for managerial, administrative or professional positions, can assist one another in job searching.

Sometimes the Country Mouse ends up in a Town Mouse situation through no fault of his own. The employer has not changed, nor even the nature of the work, but the psychological climate has altered drastically — perhaps because of a new boss three levels up, or economic adversity for the business, or even great prosperity that causes dramatic expansion. These no-fault developments happen more frequently than many realize. The gravest danger for a person who remains in the same job for a long period is not necessarily that he will atrophy in his work; it's that the climate in which he performs will change without his recognizing the metamorphosis around him.

That climate may lie further away than just the immediate environment of the company itself. When the New England textile firms went South, many employees in management were surprised and hard hit more by the change in the area than the change in their employers who continued to flourish, but in a different locale.

Sometimes instability is thrust upon an unwilling victim. Superiors insist, for whatever reason, that someone accept promotion into an unstable climate. The victim is reluctant but believes he cannot afford to refuse.

Modern Precept for Promotion: "Promotions are slower but surer in stable climates."

"Look before you leap."

The Two Frogs

Two Frogs went looking for a new home
'Cause their pond had dried only to loam.
One found a well quite deep.
His wife cried, "Wait! Don't leap."
If it dries, could we get out to roam?"

Aesop's Moral: "Look before you leap."

The Contemporary Illustration

"Now look, Kate, when you meet Mrs. Quantrell, don't call her Suzie Q. the way you have since I told you about her." Andy swerved to avoid a bicyclist riding along the edge of the road.

"Her name is Susan Quantrell, isn't it?" His wife looked absently out the car window. "I wonder why they never have sidewalks in these swanky neighborhoods?"

"You address Mrs. Quantrell as Mrs. Quantrell unless she asks you to call her Susan."

"Aye, aye, sir."

Andy threw a suspicious look her way. "Besides the Quantrells, the Harts will be there. Jane Hart's the wife. Never met her, but she's supposedly harmless. Abe Hart is executive vice president, maybe trouble. See what you think. Quantrell's title is president. He seems OK — impressive, in fact."

Kate stirred in her seat. "And of course they'll be looking me over, too. Good God, I feel like a cow on display at the state fair. Should I show my udders?"

Andy pounded the palms of his hands on the steering wheel. "Will you please try to control that kind of talk — at least for tonight while we're at this Goddam party? For my sake?"

Kate laughed and showed him a clenched fist. "Okay, tiger, I'll be in there fighting for you — in a ladylike manner, of course. Vassar, rah, rah."

"It would be good to drop in Vassar somewhere," said Andy judiciously.

"Darling, sometimes you're really funny." But she didn't laugh.

"Okay, okay, I'm uptight tonight, but this thing means a lot to me — and to you. We're on trial tonight — vice president for personnel."

"Oh come on, they want you for the job, not me. The bull is more important than the cow, just like at the state fair."

"Let's cut the agricultural figures of speech, shall we?"

"Bull shit!"

They drove the rest of the way to the Quantrells in silence.

The importance of the wives of higher management varies from company to company and from location to location. In general, the wife plays a greater role in a man's career in a smaller city than in a major metropolitan area like New York where executives live in widely dispersed areas and don't see one another too much socially. Middle-sized and smaller firms also seem to be more concerned about the wives than larger organizations. Of course, exceptions exist to both generalities.

Four ways a wife can harm her husband's career include these:

1. She has a negative attitude toward the commitments he must make to progress with the company.

Andrew had worried about this for the quarter century of their marriage. In the various jobs he had held, Kate had never been strongly committed. She had long wanted him to become a consultant; a management negotiator in bargaining with unions at smaller companies who couldn't afford experienced negotiators full time. Yet, he had never felt the time ripe to go on his own. Fortunately, she had made most of her jokes and comments in private — at least until now.

While this commitment is important in the United States, it is less so in Europe, much less so in South America and not important at all in Japan where the wife isn't expected to have any role concerning the business.

Travel and moving are the twin commitments that trouble management wives most. Fortunately, Andy had not had to do too much, although the travel potential with this new outfit could be great.

2. She behaves conspicuously while in the presence of her husband's colleagues or customers or people in the community important to his employer.

Andrew had long worried most about this. While a couple of disquieting incidents had occurred in the past, he could pin no career setbacks directly on them. He still wondered, though, if Kate's earthy language had ruined his chance to get the top personnel job with American Enterprise.

He wished Kate would not scintillate so. He would feel a lot easier if she were a mouse — much safer.

Five kinds of wives that trouble recruiters and top management are those who can't hold liquor (if they drink), those who dress too gaudily, those who are too aggressive socially, those who tend to be sexually restless or (much worse) provocative with the boss, and those who can't stand much social chitchat.

After one particularly dull social session, Andy had complimented Kate on getting through it without one four-letter Anglo-Saxonism or even an untoward remark.

"I think I've got the hang of it," she had said in triumph. "I say 'hmmmm' a couple of times and then repeat my conversational partner's last four words. I didn't utter a word of my own all night! Worked like a charm."

3. She maintains a home life that's a source of distracting harassment to her husband.

Andy couldn't really fault Kate on this. She was an amusing hostess and an efficient housewife. However, there were a few problems even here. For example, when their only child, Janet, had eloped three thousand miles to California, Kate insisted on saying in public several times, "While the ceremony was in progress, the bride's mother wore torn blue pajamas." The line had made extensive rounds among the cocktail set at American Enterprise.

But Kate was neither a free spender nor haphazard bookkeeper. She presented Andy with no financial headaches — quite the contrary. While Andy suspected that his associates speculated about the stability of his marriage, it was solid — especially since Kate had returned to work in personnel at the community hospital where they had both started in employee relations twenty-five years earlier. Although no financial need dictated her action, she had insisted upon it. And indeed it had absorbed her abundant energies and provided an income for pleasant extras. For example, Andy, even without another job immediately in the offing, had felt no compunction about resigning from American Enterprise when he had failed to get the promotion. They had even gone on a Caribbean cruise for a week, or as Kate put it, "a glorious seven days and fourteen nights."

While Andy knew that some companies frowned on careers for wives of their top managers, the question hadn't arisen thus far in his interviews for this position. It had, however, with American Enterprise. Its president had once snidely asked him if Kate's job "distracted" him. Of course not. It delighted him. American Enterprise even got edgy if the wife of a top manager had a private income — on the theory that this may dampen commitments and ambitions.

4. She can't keep up with her husband on either or both of the social and psychological planes as he moves ahead.

On this score, Andy had no complaints whatsoever. Kate knew employee relations work well and had returned to the field. In her years away from it, she had kept up with it through Andy's associations. As chief labor negotiator for American Enterprise, Andy had come to rely importantly on her advice concerning strategy and tactics. She also had a knack for getting along well with union representatives. Several had become their personal friends — largely, he acknowledged, because of Kate. "She talks our language," one tough union official had once told Andy in surprise.

Kate's language was the subject for discussion as the pair were driving back home from the Quantrell's dinner party that night.

"Your choice of words wasn't the most elevated tonight, my dear," said Andy. "I don't think the word 'screw' gets much usage in the Quantrell living room in the context you used it."

"I'm sorry, honey, but you know what a stuffed-shirt atmosphere does to me. I just can't stand it. I want to shake them up."

"And that story didn't go over well about how you had to visit the gynecologist to make sure you weren't pregnant after the Caribbean cruise."

Kate smiled. "Hart almost split his gut, and Quantrell couldn't stop laughing."

"But the wives didn't approve, and they were the important ones tonight. They didn't like your smoking the little cigars either."

Kate lit one now. "Andy, I switched from cigarets to cigars when I saw later in the evening that this job was not for you."

"I would appreciate having some say in whether it's for me or not."

"No, no," she said hastily. "I mean that you would not have gotten along with either Hart or Quantrell. You yourself said earlier that Hart's a bastard. You're right. Look at the way he treats his wife. Cutting off her drinks after one martini, for heaven's sake. Openly embarrassing her when Quantrell went to fill her glass. And that knowing leer from Quantrell. It made me sick. But Quantrell would be even worse — pompous, vain. Did you see how he was always shooting his cuffs and smoothing that snow-white hair of his? And ideas! The last new one he had was in 1939. He would make life hell for you in labor negotiations. No wonder they're in so much trouble with their union."

They rode in silence for a while. "Darling," she said quietly. "I wish you'd give some hard thought to consulting. You know the hospital would take you on in two minutes for their negotiating. And that group of tool and die shops has asked you several times. With what I make at the hospital and your fees, we'd do fine financially, especially now that Janet's gone."

Andy put his hand on her knee. "Let's sleep on it."

She put her hand over his.

Modern Precept for Promotion: "Your spouse can serve as a sounding board to help in your career and career decisions."

"Some characters have no sense
of obligation."

The Ungrateful Wolf

Crane drew a kid's bone from the Wolf's throat,
Then for services a sum did quote.
Snarled Wolf: "I'll pay no charge.
Your bill is much too large.
Give thanks I don't eat you like the goat."

Aesop's Moral: "Some characters have no sense of obligation."

The Contemporary Illustration

Grant Bristol closed his eyes as he started to dictate a letter to his most troublesome tenant. The closed eyes gave Grant's face a defenseless, small-boy look, Zoe Masters mused. She always thought of him as Grant, although she of course addressed him as Mr. Bristol.

He usually closed his eyes while dictating, and he seldom looked at her directly, although she knew that he often watched her when he thought she was unaware of his attention. She found him diffident, oddly appealing and a little pathetic, too. Take this letter. He should not send a letter. He should go see Mr. Goff. The man was only two floors below, for heaven's sake. His complaint about the elevator service should be thrashed out, face to face.

"Don't you think you should see Mr. Goff instead of writing this letter?" Zoe surprised herself by voicing her thoughts.

Grant opened his eyes and looked directly at her. The suggestion had accomplished something, anyway.

"Zoe, let me do things my way. My father may have charged in to see Goff. I may have to do it yet, but we'll try the letter first. OK?"

"Of course, Mr. Bristol." She felt the color rising because Grant had read another of her thoughts, a little deeper down. Mr. Bristol, Sr. would indeed have handled Goff directly. She had been the father's secretary for three years and had known his methods. Business and personal. She had not minded — actually had enjoyed — his frank admiration and frequent compliments about her appearance. But the admiration and compliments had never gone beyond the bounds of good sense.

He had played the role of the wolf, but he had actually been a lamb. She missed him. Since his death, his son Grant had taken over managing the building. Now everything was different, mixed up — including her feelings for the new boss.

"I'm sorry, Mr. Bristol, I missed that part."

Grant opened his eyes again. "Zoe, you're not yourself today."

"Maybe not."

"What's wrong?"

"Nothing really. Well, yes, there is. I was thinking about your father. I know every person does things differently. You have your methods for running this building. He had his." She waved her steno pad. "I'm not criticizing, but I wouldn't take any more of this guff from Goff, even if he is the biggest tenant."

"Is that what Dad called it, 'guff from Goff'?"

She smiled. "Yes and a lot of even less polite things."

He frowned. "Well, Dad could afford to be high handed with Goff. He carried the guy for three years during the depression when his publishing business wasn't making a dime."

She shrugged. "Honest, I don't think this letter will help at all. The direct approach is right for him, face to face."

He sat looking at her, the longest direct appraisal he had ever given her. "You think I let him browbeat me?"

"Yes sir," she said firmly.

Another pause. Then he smiled faintly. "So do I. We'll have no more guff from Goff. Call him; see if he's in. If he is, tell him I'm on my way to see him. I don't want to talk to him on the phone."

"Yes sir!" Zoe dialed the number from memory, learned Goff was in, nodded to Grant, smiled as he got up. "Good luck," she called and blew a kiss to his retreating back.

He returned in less than an hour, and her heart sank as she saw him.

"The bastard!" he waved a sheet of paper. "Handed me a list of things wrong with the building. Had it waiting for me — like a wolf lurking in his cave. He looks like a wolf glowering behind that mammoth desk of his. An ungrateful wolf. I reminded the bastard of those three years my father carried him. He just laughed at me. And speaking of gratitude, I shall be everlastingly grateful to you, Miss Masters, for shaming me into facing Goff in his lair."

She couldn't help it, but began to cry as soon as he had gone into his own office.

In a moment she jumped. His hand was on her shoulder.

"I'm sorry Zoe. I shouldn't have said that. Of course, I had to see him in person. You were absolutely right." He handed her a handkerchief and she dried her tears.

"Let me see that list of ultimatums the ungrateful wolf gave you," she said at last. She nodded as she read them over. "I have to admit he's got some valid gripes here. The elevators are museum pieces, unmodernized since they were installed a half century ago. No central air conditioning. Routine maintenance behind schedule.

He nodded gloomily as he lit a cigaret, handed it lit to her and lit another for himself. She felt half amused and half thrilled. He took her hand "What in the hell are we going to do?"

"The first thing is that *we...*" She emphasized the pronoun. "...aren't going to run this building on gratitude. Your father did — or on something certainly not money. He didn't put a dime in it that he didn't have to since he took over from his own father in the Depression."

"I know," said Grant. "He was close with the dollar. Hell, I never wanted to run this dump." He looked around in distaste.

"Perhaps you could sell out?"

He shook his head. "The capital gain would kill Mother from the tax standpoint. The income from here is what she lives on."

"Look," she said, turning to face him more directly but not removing her hand from his. "This building could be a real money-maker again if it were modernized. This section of town's perking up now that Amalgamated has built its new headquarters down the block. How about trying for a modernization loan?"

"Yes, I've thought of that." He sounded doubtful. "But I don't know a thing about construction, renovation, that kind of thing."

"But you could learn. Banks help on things like that. And aren't there office building consultants whom you could hire?" She paused, glancing at their hands still clasped. "*We* could learn, Grant."

"I *am* grateful to you, Miss Masters. He smiled as he looked at their hands. "I'm the grateful wolf."

She looked down. "When is the grateful wolf going to do more than hold my hand?"

Modern Precept for Promotion: "You can't base your business career on the gratitude of others."

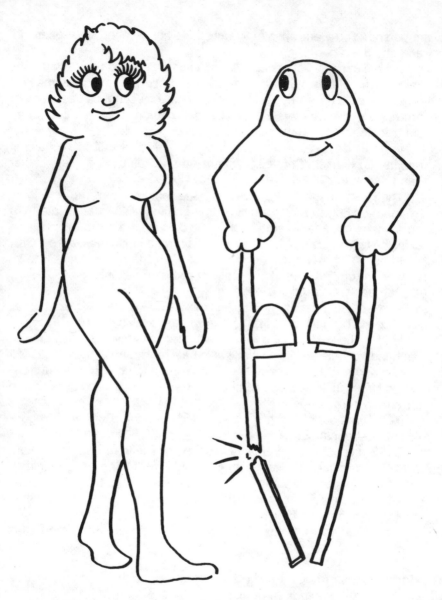

"Borrowed plumes are soon discovered."

The Vain Jackdaw

Jack borrowed plumes to meet with the fowls.
Then a question was raised by the owls
Whose very wise old eyes
Soon saw through his disguise.
So Jackdaw had to flee from the howls.

Aesop's Moral: "Borrowed plumes are soon discovered."

The Contemporary Illustration

Hugh Z. guiltily put aside the *Times* crossword puzzle as Mary trailed into the family room, cigaret in mouth, coffee cup in her left hand and her right waving a copy of the *Wall Street Journal*. "Herz un ya didna mark."

"What?"

She put the coffee cup on an end table, removed the cigaret from her mouth and pointed at a help-wanted ad. "This ad. You didn't mark it."

Hugh peered at the classifieds and read:

MAVERICKS

If you're not satisfied with promotion possibilities
or bored with your current situation and looking
for action, read on. . .

As the fastest growing company in our field of transportation, we need aggressive, dynamic individuals
to move quickly into responsible marketing positions.
A Mechanical Engineering Degree and business/sales-
engineering experience are helpful but not necessary —
creativity and mechanical aptitude can substitute.

In addition to the chance to move up fast, we offer a
salary commensurate with your qualifications, excellent fringe benefits and a convenient Long Island
location. Reply in confidence to . . . .

Hugh sighed and picked up the crossword puzzle. "Of course I didn't mark that one. It doesn't fit for me. I marked those two." He indicated two other "position available" ads for mechanical engineers. "I've already sent resumes in the mail this morning."

Mary flicked cigaret ashes which fell into her coffee cup. Unconcerned, she took a sip. "Sure, those are alright. But this one sounds interesting. Why not send your resume to it, too? What can you lose?"
"Eight cents in postage — and the aggravation of hearing nothing whatsoever as a result of the mailing. If I sent that one out, it would be the one hundred and seventh I've mailed. All for nothing."

"Oh come on, Hughie. They've generated interviews from four companies. And Amalgamated said they probably will call you back."

"But I've heard nothing in ten days. Probably another big fat zero. Nothing in more than three months of looking — really four months, because I started a month before Ajax laid me off when I could already see the handwriting on the wall."

Mary took another sip of coffee and made a face as she tasted cigaret ash. "Maybe you're looking in the wrong places, honey. Shift your sights — to something like this 'maverick' ad."

"That's a selling job." Hugh threw down the puzzle. "I'm an engineer, not a salesman."

"Nonsense. You can sell. Look at all those trips you made for Ajax to customers' plants."

"Those were debugging trips, getting the equipment to work right."

"Well, that's selling isn't it? Keeping the Ajax equipment sold, you always said, was harder than selling it at the beginning."

"It's not the same," said Hugh in the tone he used in helping Hugh, Jr. with his twelfth-grade math homework. "This job is not for me. I'm Hugh Average, every man's engineer, not Hugh Maverick, dynamic and aggressive."

This time Mary threw down her paper. "There you go again. Downgrading yourself. You know what maverick means? Dissenter. And if you aren't a dissenter, I don't know what you are. You dissent from everything I have to suggest. Maverick also means orphaned. And if a guy out of a job doesn't feel orphaned, I don't know what he feels."

She was crying as she fled from the room.

A few minutes later he came into their bedroom where she was lying face-down on the bed. "Mary, OK I'm a maverick. I'm going to mail this outfit my resume." He showed her the envelope. She took it and tore it in half.

"For God's sake." He struck his forehead in half-mocking dismay. "Now what's wrong?"

"Let's redo this resume, to emphasize the selling experience you've had. Let's make out you've been selling since you left your mother's knee."

If you've not thought about it, you may have missed the fact that getting a job is a matter of selling yourself to a boss. When you are selling something, you want to be sure you are representing the product, (yourself), in terms of the customer's (the potential employer's) interests, while still telling the truth.

I suggest a do-it-at-home vocational guidance exercise, much abbreviated. If you want general aptitude testing and counselling, check with one of the local universities or state professional employment service.

For a short-form self-appraisal, let's start thinking about things, events, or situations in your previous jobs, training, and outside activities that have prepared you for the jobs you held. What is there about these previous experiences that has significance relative to your proposed move? What things have you done of a constructive nature that turned out well? What would you say were your real accomplishments? The answers to these will provide you with valuable information about what you can do well — what you've got to sell to that new boss. They will also help you identify areas of weakness that ought either to be avoided or compensated for if your product is going to be a success in the marketplace.

Refer to the fable of the "Peacock's Complaint" for specific tips on self-appraisal.

I have been talking a lot about assets and achievements but do not forget the problem areas. Everyone has limitations; successful people recognize these and adjust accordingly — so analyze your data and determine what problems and mistakes have been critical in your career to date. These are your limitations. Keep them in mind as you consider new assignments.

Next you have to have a sales brochure or resume. Use the self-appraisal analysis as a basis for such a document. Check your product against these guidelines.

1. Keep it short and in plain English, avoid using jargon that will not be understood outside your department or business.

2. Support the strengths you have identified by being selective in what you choose to write about. Let the figures (or other quantifiers and qualifiers) speak for themselves.

3. Stress your contributions to profits, the success of your component, etc., within the framework of assigned responsibilities.

4. If you are looking for a managerial position, keep in mind the basic skills of managing — hiring, training, motivating, measuring, and sometimes firing people. Include your success in these activities through your contributions.

5. Remember that you are trying to sell your ability to accomplish

some tangible things — to increase profits, improve productivity, solve technical problems. Use action verbs such as "managed", "developed", "organized", etc.

When Hugh completed his best effort, he showed it to his wife, asking her to check it for ambiguous language, misspellings and the like. Grammatical errors can detract from the effectiveness of the document.

While Mary found no problems in those areas, she wasn't satisfied in others. "It still doesn't sell hard enough. Let's put in how you led the church's fund-raising campaign last year. That's the hardest selling there is, and you went over the goal 3 per cent."

The revised document finally went out. Three days later, Hugh received a phone call and an invitation to come for an interview with a firm only 20 miles away that made equipment for truck trailers. A date was set for the following Monday.

When she heard, Mary said, "Good, you can borrow Hugh, Jr.'s suit, the double-knit job. You're not only going to be a maverick; you're going to look like one."

For the interview, he also borrowed from Hugh, Jr. a red and grey striped shirt and a maroon tie, in contrast to his usual white shirt and conservative dark tie.

"Mary, I feel like I'm going there under false colors." He surveyed himself on the morning of the interview in the mirror on the back of the closet door. "This isn't the real me."

"It's the new you, and the real you from now on." She kissed him as he turned to go to the car. "Good luck in the interview."

The interview is *the* most important activity in your search for a new job. Everything you've done so far has been designed solely to produce the interview. Your performance in the interview will be the key to getting hired for the job you want. It will be helpful if you think of an employment interview as an information exchange process between you and a perspective employer. It requires equilibrium (a balanced exchange of ideas) for success and should prepare both parties for a decision.

The term "process" implies a series of related actions. It is important to realize that you will be an active participant in the process, *not* a passive subject. Therefore, you should be prepared to play your part. Most situations where you and another person get together to exchange data or ideas are a form of interview — meeting with a potential customer to sell a product, business review with your boss, problem resolution with a peer, etc. You should approach the employment interview with the same preparation and plans for participation.

Maintaining a balanced dialogue is important to the process. Neither party should dominate. Since you will both ask and answer questions, you will have to be prepared for both if you are going to be successful.

One way in which you lose balance is to lag the question. You are asked question #1; you answer it. You are asked question #2; you start to answer, but realize that you haven't said all you wanted to say in question #1. Your mind is still partially answering #1, but you are trying to answer #2. The same happens with #2 while you are trying to answer #3. By the time you get to question #5, you have lost your balance and probably the interview as well.

You need your faculties to determine the timing and degree of your responses (i.e., to maintain equilibrium); therefore, you must have the basic data carefully stored away before hand.

Another way that you lose your balance is by losing your confidence. Your attitude and outlook are important here. The preparation you have done to get an interview should give you confidence when you enter the interview situation — provided of course that you have prepared objectively and honestly.

The prospective employer needs to gather as much data about you as he can. You need to gather as much data about him, the business, and the industry as you can. Therefore, you must be prepared to tell him what he needs to know and ask him what you need to know. For what he and you will want to know, see the fable of the "Sick Lion and the Ass."

A word about the interviewer. As a practical matter, you will be faced with only two kinds of interviewers — skilled and unskilled. They require slightly different kinds of effort on your part.

Skillful interviewing is usually the result of significant training and practice. Most operating managers do not have the time to become skilled interviewers.

You can spot the unskilled interviewer because he tends to talk much more than he listens and frequently doesn't know what to ask you. This is a very dangerous situation because that unskilled interviewer is going to make a decision about you regardless of the volume or value of the data he collects.

In this situation the only way you can fulfill the obligation of an interview — exchange data, maintain equilibrium and reach a good decision — is if you are prepared to carry the ball and do carry it. You will have to be looking for entry points to volunteer your assets and accomplishments and ask what you need to know. This will help generate the needed data exchange.

On the other hand, I hope that the preparation you have done makes dealing with a skilled interviewer a pleasant task. He knows what to ask you; he will get the data needed for a decision. You should sit back, relax and give him your story as he asks for it. Listen to the question and answer it as asked. Be specific and to the point.

The favorite technique of the skillful interviewer is to check for consistency. He will ask you the same question in several different ways: "Tell me why you got promoted?" and "What are your assets?" With questions he looks for your strengths, but the inquiries probably will come at different times and not appear to be asking the same thing.

Hugh had a skillful interviewer.

"I don't really see much sales engineering experience here," he mused. "We called you in, hoping that there would be a little more than what showed in the resume."

"Well, I've done a lot of debugging work — after-sale selling." Hugh tried to put confidence into the comment, but he felt his conviction ebbing, especially as the interviewer said nothing. "And there was the church drive I headed."

"That would be more on the administrative side wouldn't it — at least from the experience I have had in those affairs."

The interviewer made the comment more as a statement than a question. Now, Hugh had nothing to say. The interview went downhill from then on, and Hugh left with a feeling of having been caught with his hand in the cookie jar. He had been neither objective nor honest in preparing for this interview, thrown off-center by his wife's pleas.

On his way home, he rehearsed some caustic comments to make to Mary. But he forgot them because she met him, radiant, at the door.

"Darling, a man from Amalgamated just called. He apologized for the delay; everybody has been tied up in some kind of big engineering department meeting. But they want to see you again, and you have a date for tomorrow morning."

As Hugh was changing his clothes and hanging up the double-knit suit, he said, "I think I'll wear my blue pinstripe tomorrow."

"Good," said Mary. "I'll get it pressed."

Hugh fingered the double-knit reflectively. "In the excitement about Amalgamated, Mary, I forgot to say that the maverick interview didn't pan out."

Mary took the pinstripe and hurried out of the room. "It's all for the best, darling. You're no maverick."

Modern Precept for Promotion: "You advance when you put your merits in the light that best — and most honestly — reflects you."

"Persuasion is better than force."

The Wind and the Sun

The Wind and the Sun made a bet:
The traveller's coat which should get.
Blew the Wind — the coat clung.
Shone the Sun — the coat flung.
So the Sun had the best of it yet.

Aesop's Moral: "Persuasion is better than force."

The Contemporary Illustration

The automotive parts manufacturer experienced trouble with quality. The president wrote editorials on the subject in the employee newspaper. He called a meeting of all hourly employees and warned of the dire results to the company and their jobs if workmanship didn't improve.

Little improvement resulted until Dan K., the general superintendent, tried a different approach. He wrote to the National Safety Council and to police departments in several cities and states, asking for authenticated cases of automobile accidents which were proved to have been caused by defective parts. From the press he gathered dramatic examples of other parts failures — for example, a faulty thirty-nine-cent fastener which caused the failure of a multimillion-dollar guided missile, the defective welding suspected as the cause of the loss of the atomic submarine *Thresher*. He kept a scrapbook of these horrible examples also, and he stored some of the clippings in his pocket. When the occasion seemed right, he showed his scrapbook or his individual clippings to some of his people, rarely more than two or three at a time. He didn't lecture or moralize. He let the examples do that for him. He continued the practice for weeks.

"This proved more effective in improving quality than all the editorials and harangues put together," Dan reported. His performance helped win him a promotion to plant manager.

Nor does cynicism help noticeably in persuading people to your point of view. Carl M., foreman on a line of women assembling electric can openers, told the girls things like this: "Give everything you've got to this can opener, gals, or you'll all have to listen to Mr. Big's big mouth." Or:

"Put a little more heart into this, kids. America needs more electric can openers."

The cynicism amused some for a while, but it soon paled. Carl didn't last long as foreman.

In contrast, Joan C. was supervisor over girls operating machines that assembled light bulbs. "We make light for sight" she would tell them. In admonishing one employee for sloppy inspection, she said, "You let one go by that could explode. That might put someone's eye out."

Her unabashedly emotional approach worked. She supervised the best line in the company, and eventually became general foreman. Her comment, "light for sight," became an advertising slogan.

Some supervisors are reticent about expressing enthusiasm concerning the dignity of work, the values of friendship and are inarticulate in finding the words to express appreciation and admiration.

American folklore which honors the "strong, silent type," may account for this inhibition in many supervisors. The problem seems more acute among men than women, which could explain why women often make excellent supervisors. Emotions tend to mirror themselves. Carl's cynicism bred cynicism. Joan's sincerity bred its counterpart.

Paternalism is another form of force that doesn't persuade readily, either. The boss's daughter worked for the summer in the stenographic pool. Sarah L., the pool's supervisor, showed such obvious favoritism toward her that she had demoralized the entire operation by the end of the summer. She imagined she was impressing the boss for future favorable notice from him. Instead, she had to leave because she could no longer supervise the steno pool effectively.

When the union organizers came around trying to persuade draftsman to join the American Federation of Technical Employees, Dick Y., the manager of drafting, realized that this constituted a threat to his ambitions of being promoted to manager of engineering. He hastened to assure his boss that the draftsmen generally were sympathetic to management and would vote for no union.

"Just a couple of hotheads have stirred up the trouble," he said.

Yet the draftsmen voted overwhelmingly in favor of the union. And Dick lost as well — both the non-union status of his unit and his hopes for promotion.

Professor Howard Boone Jacobson, chairman of the Department of Industrial Journalism at the University of Bridgeport, believes that the nature of the white-collar employee's work is becoming more and more like that of his fellows on the assembly line. He believes that as the white-collarite finds he must conform more rigidly than ever to the new computer-controlled program he has been assigned, his ideas about social identification, loyalties and job security have changed.

His survey of 117 corporations with an average work force of 10,869, 33.7 per cent of them salaried, shows that the attitudes of many managers toward unionism among white-collarites are dangerously complacent.

"You cannot convince a white-collar employee that he is a part of the management team if he has no decisions to make and is completely isolated from the decision-makers," he comments.

But Dick ignored this advice, at his cost in the promotional sweepstakes.

While complacency won't prove permanently persuasive, neither will its opposite, aggressiveness. Howard G., in football parlance, had drive, desire and ability. And he knew it. Six months after joining the editorial staff of a magazine, he asked the editor for a $100-a-month raise and promotion to the Washington bureau which had an opening at the time. Amused and impressed, the editor did move him to Washington — at a $25 monthly increase. Less than a year later, the bureau chief died unexpectedly from a heart attack. Howard immediately asked for the job. Not so amused this time, the editor temporized. Howard was only twenty-five years old and had been on the staff less than eighteen months. He offered the post to a more experienced staffer who refused because his wife didn't want to move to Washington.

The editor made an offer to a seasoned writer on a rival publication. He turned it down. Finally, the editor gave the nod to Howard. As the months rolled on, the Washington bureau chief confounded his critics on the staff, who had grown to formidable numbers by this time, by performing creditably although sometimes erratically. He had misinterpreted the facts in a couple of news developments and had misquoted powerful government officials on several occasions.

While these gaffes caused the editor considerable distress when he learned of them, particularly one that Howard had attempted to cover up, he kept the young man in Washington because he had also scored a number of scoops.

However, when he discovered that Howard had gone behind his back to the publisher and asked for his own job, he flew to Washington and fired Howard.

If you tend to excuse Howard because of brash inexperience, reconsider. He had actually approached the publisher twice with the same proposition. After the second episode, the publisher decided that enough was enough and advised the editor to discharge the bureau chief.

Aggressive, but more experienced people can run into trouble too. Nate C., a veteran civil servant in a federal agency, used powerful political friends to win promotion to the second highest post in the organization — which technically could be a political appointment but which by custom had long gone to career people in the civil service. But Nate could not get the job through customary channels; that's why he resorted to politics.

"The name of the game in politics is influence," he explained. "Why shouldn't I use it when I had it?"

Why indeed? The problem was that Nate's agency colleagues began to make his life miserable because he hadn't played the game as they thought it should be played — through the civil service. In his new and exalted position, he found that he could get little cooperation. Mysterious delays and snags developed in the projects he backed. He found himself ostracized by the civil service people with whom he had once socialized.

Within a year, Nate gave up. He retired early from government service.

Modern Precept for Promotion: "You may cause yourself more trouble than advancement by trying to bull your way to the top."

"Fraud and violence have no scruples."

The Wolf and the Lamb

Wolf seized Lamb, saying, "You're the winner!"
"Of what?" cried the Lamb. "I'm a sinner."
Mused Wolf: "Perhaps that's true,
But you're easy to chew.
So I prefer lamb for my dinner."

Aesop's Moral: "Fraud and violence have no scruples."

The Contemporary Illustration

For his first job after college, Wade J. joined the sales promotion department of a cosmetic firm. He had worked there for a year before he even faintly suspected that his boss had flexible ethics.

The suspicion was conceived at a Christmas party at his manager's swank New York apartment where he saw on the walls the artwork for the firm's recent advertising campaign — all expensive original paintings by well-known artists. The suspicion came to life shortly afterward. The boss's secretary had been out ill, and Wade had taken a call for her from the accounting department asking about a bill from something named Promotion Consultors, Inc. In rummaging through her records to try to find an answer, he found the firm's file, but it clarified nothing. He asked the manager.

"Oh that," he replied. "Leave it to me; I'll handle it."

"What is Promotion Consultors?" Wade asked.

"I use them for sales ideas," said the boss offhandedly. Yet Wade had never seen any representatives from Promotion Consultors in the office and knew nothing about what it contributed. As the firm was nearby, as indicated by the address in its file, he investigated during a lunch hour. Its name appeared on the lobby directory of a seedy Manhattan building.

That might have satisfied Wade, but a nagging doubt remained. The building didn't look like the quarters for an outfit that his boss usually retained. His taste went to flamboyant and glossy vendors, not hole-and-corner firms like this.

Wade took the rickety elevator to the fourth floor. At room 410, four names straggled down the frosted glass panel of the door, including an accountant, Promotion Consultants, Inc., Creative Printing, Inc., and American Advertising Specialties. Except for the accountant, Wade recognized them all from files he had seen while hunting for the answer to the Promotion Consultants' question.

When he reached for the doorknob, he found the door locked. He knocked, not expecting any response, but he was surprised to hear a stirring. The door opened a crack, to reveal the right eye and part of the elaborate hairdo of a woman.

"How do you do," said Wade. "I'm looking for someone from Promotion Consultants."

"They're out to lunch," said the woman in a husky voice.

"Oh, I'm wondering if they could help me — on a product idea I have." Wade was annoyed to find himself sweating, although it was winter and the hall cold.

"They're quite busy now — all the work they can handle, I'm afraid."

"Oh, well, perhaps I can find someone else — in the *Yellow Pages*."

The woman said nothing for a moment. "Is that where you found us, in the *Yellow Pages*?"

"Ah, yes."

Wade turned and left for the elevator, disturbed. He recognized that elaborate, piled-up hairdo and the husky voice as belonging to a woman whom he met at the boss's Christmas party. And he had an uneasy feeling that he would not find Promotion Consultants listed in the *Yellow Pages*. He mentally cursed himself for not checking before he had come to room 410.

Sure enough, the *Yellow Pages* did not list Promotion Consultants, nor Creative Printing, nor American Advertising Specialties, nor A.H. Smith, the accountant named on the door panel. He found them all, however, in the white-page directory, with different phone numbers but the same addresses expressed variously. One was given as an East Forty-fifth Street number, one as a building name, the third as a Second Avenue address and the fourth as Forty-fifth Street and Second Avenue. Wade had noted that the building stood on the corner and could rate either street designation.

Wade turned his suspicison into certainty when he called the accounting department and asked for the latest endorsed checks paid to the three firms — giving as an excuse the possibility of a payment mixup. The three checks had been negotiated through different banks but they were endorsed A.H. Smith, A. Haring Smith and Arlette H. Smith, respectively. He couldn't remember the name of the husky-voiced woman he had met at the Christmas party, but he bet it had been Arlette Smith.

Now that Wade virtually knew that his boss dealt with at least three dummy firms, he didn't know what to do about the situation.

Basically, an employee has five courses open to him when he encounters fraud.

First, he can entertain suspicions, but have no proof. Albert J. (in the fable of the "Hare and the Tortoise") found himself in that position. He thought Jim R., the persuasive president of the conglomerate which had bought his firm, was up to something shady, but he didn't know precisely what. Fortunately, he was given an almost completely free hand to run his own operation, which he did honestly and well. He succeeded in almost fully dissociating himself with Jim and his small coterie of wheeler-dealers and emerged to pick up the conglomerate's pieces when Jim went to jail.

Second, you can have virtual proof, but pretend that fraud doesn't exist and try to go along with your private honesty untarnished. Ben K. (in the "Fox and the Crow") attempted that course, but after six months he couldn't live with himself and the fraudulent practices that he saw going on at the little bank to which he had been lured with the title of vice president.

He learned that he could get his old job back with the legitimate bank, so he told the president of the small bank of his decision to resign. The interview proved unexpectedly difficult.

"I don't understand," said the bank's chief smoothly. "We made you vice president, as promised. Everything's going well, at least from my viewpoint. Why do you want to leave after only six months?"

"I've decided that I'm not suited for this work," said Ben who had rehearsed the answer.

"But you're doing fine. As I say, I'm pleased. So's everyone else on the board."

"Well, I'm not at ease in this kind of work."

The president held up his hands in a supplicating gesture. "Please give it a longer and fairer trial. You aren't being fair to us, leaving so soon."

"No, no, I'm sorry. I can't stay. My old job's waiting for me."

The president sat for a moment and then stood up. "As you know, much activity in all banking, including in ours, is confidential. I would hate to believe that you would reveal any of our confidential matters to outsiders."

Ben jumped up like a jack-in-the-box. "Of course not. Not a word. I wouldn't think of it."

The president ushered Ben to the door. "And how is your family? Your wife Jean is a lovely woman. And Pauline, I understand, will be going away to college this fall. Boston University, is it?"

"Yes," said Ben, surprised at the non sequitur and puzzled because he had never mentioned his family at the bank.

"I hope they remain happy and healthy," said the president without smiling. He gripped Ben's hand so hard that it felt sore for the next three days. Ben did return to his old job, and revealed no secrets. His wife and daughter remained healthy, at least, but neither was happy at the slow change in Ben. In his mid-forties he looked sixty.

The third course is to join wholeheartedly in the fraud, hoping also to benefit personally. Dave G. did that (in "the Snake and the File") when he became a willing ally of his sales manager in the boss's hanky-panky with his secretary and in the maneuvers to rid themselves of Greg Z. who knew too much and talked too much. Dave's triumph proved short-lived, however, because the whole sales department was reorganized after a year of poor performances. Dave was forced to take an early retirement.

The fourth course relates to the first — leave the job immediately upon discovering the violence or the fraud, but say nothing to avoid trouble. Belle Y. bullied Sally T., the gentle science teacher in the "Dog in the Manger," and also falsified her performance appraisals so that she was not rehired. Sally knew of the bullying, of course, and suspected the falsifying, but she did not complain to the principal and meekly left the job.

Wade took the fifth course, although he was tempted seriously to follow the third and go along with the fraud. For a while, Wade did nothing except tell his fiancée about his findings. She urged him to report to the cosmetic firm's president immediately. Wade didn't do that at once, but investigated further. He learned that Arlette Smith, indeed, was an accountant. She was unmarried. And, another piece fell in place when he learned that she had an apartment in the same building as his boss. And the key piece turned up when Wade learned that both Arlette and the manager had worked together for another cosmetic firm years before.

Still, Wade did nothing. One day, the boss called him into his sumptuous office.

"Wade, I notice from your vacation request that you want to take it this year in April."

"Yes, I'm getting married. Honeymoon."

"Congratulations!" The manager got up and shook his hand vigorously. "Wade, I have a little suggestion. We need to research our

French perfume competitors. Learn the latest sales promotion gimmicks they're using. How would you like to go to Paris, look into things? And of course take your honeymoon at the same time." The boss looked at him from under his thick eyebrows. "Of course, we might even manage to pick up part of the tab for your new wife."

"Gosh, that sounds wonderful, sir. We had planned Bermuda." Wade, not anticipating this approach, retired in confusion. "I'll have to ask my fiancée."

"Naturally, but there should be no trouble cancelling for Bermuda and getting your money back at this date. It's only February, two months to go."

That night, his fiancée was indignant. "It's a bribe! Can't you see that, Wade? I'll bet he's bought lots of people off around your shop, hasn't he?"

Wade had considered that possibility. His prime candidate for being in on the deal, besides the boss, was the secretary, whose absence because of illness had precipitated his investigations.

The next day he called the company's president from a pay phone. With some difficulty, he got an appointment for later that morning.

The president listened without saying a word as Wade told the story, showed him copies of the dummy companies' bills, the peculiar listings in the telephone directory and the check endorsements with the name variations and identical handwriting.

"These charges are serious," the president said. "I must have them investigated. That may take a while." He paused and gazed meditatively out the window. "In the meantime, we don't want him to become alarmed. Where does he think you are now?"

"I said I had a dental appointment and wouldn't be in until after lunch."

The president nodded. "That ought to be all right — unless he happened to see you coming in here."

"That's unlikely. He has been in an ad conference all morning."

The president nodded again. "That's good. Another thing — when you go into your office after lunch, see him and accept that Paris trip. Let him think he's bought you. Be obsequious with him. Can you manage that?"

"I think so." Wade shifted at a sudden thought. "But sir, what if he goes ahead and makes reservations, buys tickets for Paris and so on."

"So much the better. We'll have that much more on him." The president smiled for the first time during the interview. "You may even take that sales-promotion-cum-honeymoon trip to France — at my expense."

Wade and his bride did honeymoon in Paris — and even did a little sales promotion study for the firm. The suspected fraud investigation turned up far more than had been suspected. Besides receiving payment for nonexistent work supposedly performed for the cosmetic firm, the three dummy companies also served as the funnel through which the manager had been receiving kickbacks from legitimate printers, ad agencies and other vendors. The ex-boss, his secretary and Arlette had milked the company of nearly half a million dollars over nine years.

Modern Precept for Promotion: "You can't win real promotions through dishonesty."

"Appearances may be deceptive."

The Wolf in Sheep's Clothing

A wily wolf, the lambs to win,
Clad himself to look like their kin,
Until a shepherd lad,
A recent college grad,
Choked him on his new sheepskin.

Aesop's Moral: "Appearances may be deceptive."

The Contemporary Illustration

People often don't get what they bargain for when they seize an apparent promotional opportunity with another employer. The same phenomenon can also occur within a company, although less often.

Dr. Jerome C. Beam, vice president of Psychological Services at Clark, Channell, Inc., believes that the corporate environment determines the kind of qualities a man must have to succeed. Some sociologists go even further and contend that success does not reside so much in a person as in the organization's environment. Environment varies according to industry, company, department within a company, and even units within a department.

Bert S. moved from editor of a managers' newsletter in Corporate Employee Relations to manager of non-union relations within the same operation. In six months, he returned with relief to the editorship of the newsletter. His "promotion" within the same department had failed.

In the non-union situation he found himself in a high-pressure atmosphere. The idea was to keep as many components non-union as possible. When two voted to become organized by unions, the losses almost tore Bert apart. He discovered he much preferred to report on such events in his newsletter than to be part of the news-making event itself.

Or the promotional situation may require personal characteristics you aren't strong in. Frederick Gaudet and A.R. Carli, psychologists, asked 177 top executives why they had failed to promote somebody or why, having promoted him, he proved a disappointment. The respondents stated that personality factors were the most important reason for failure by a ratio of 11 to 1 over know-how.

The five most frequently cited reasons were in order: "Inability to delegate responsibility . . . Lack of breadth of knowledge (overspecialization) . . . Inability to analyze and evaluate . . . Inability to judge people . . . Inability to cooperate with others."

Besides being uneasy in the new environment, Bert had personality defects that led to his failure in the non-union job. He couldn't delegate responsibility. After years of being an individual contributor as editor of the newsletter, he found he tried to do everything himself. Because too much needed doing, he failed to accomplish all that his job required. Furthermore, the people who nominally reported to him had too little to do, except mischief, which they proceeded to make in back-biting activities against their harrassed boss.

Bert had no trouble with a third deceptive appearance that surprises many recently promoted people: The job is not as advertised. Max T. was promoted to become sales manager in New York City for an office equipment manufacturer. He foresaw the higher costs and other negative factors of living in New York. But one offsetting factor (he thought) would be the lessened need for travel. He understood that his territory included New York City only, but he soon discovered how wrong that was. Some of his New York-based customers had plants or other facilities in out-of-the-way places where his firm, a relatively small outfit, had no sales representation.

So, the inevitable happened. He had to visit customer facilities in such places as Hookset, New Hampshire; Suburn, Maine; and Washingtonville, Pennsylvania. He found himself travelling as much as he ever had. Eventually, it became too much for him; he quit.

Sometimes the misconceptions about job descriptions arise because of the blinders that you wear.

A common self-blinder results from the large raise that the promotion would seemingly bring. The high cost of New York City is so well-known that few would fail to take it into consideration, but other areas hold similar pitfalls. For example, investigate the tax aspects of that promotion into the Canadian subsidiary. Canadian tax structures will take a 10 per cent deeper bite than U.S. levies from a manager earning $25,000 or more annually. Or the move to Podunk Center may seem beneficial statistically — except for one thing. The public schools are so poor that you must send your children to expensive private institutions.

A fourth and related area of misconceptions grows out of diminishing satisfaction. It could result from managerial mobility, for example. As you start your career, you may enjoy the move to a new location. Both the promotion and new surroundings prove stimulating — but probably not after the fifteenth or twentieth time.

Of the 40 million people who move each year in the United States, more than half are involved in company transfers. A recent survey showed that some 68 per cent of the nation's managers and professionals in the twenty-five to forty age range move at least once every three years, 23 per cent move every two years and 18 per cent move annually.

IBM's policy of shifting people around the world generated the quip that its initials stand for "I've been moved."

While IBM and other firms are reportedly trying to cut down on corporate mobility, the practice persists as a way of life, and its attractions may pall after the first few experiences with it.

Another species of diminishing satisfaction develops when the new job turns out to be bound into a diminishing environment. Some competent, even brilliant people get lured through ignorance, cupidity or conceit into apparent promotions during the declining days of failures. Art A. was an instant hero when he pledged to save the foundry, Podunk's last remaining industry. But high transportation costs and obsolete facilities had already doomed the enterprise. He soon became the villain as the foundry slid into inevitable bankruptcy. Art's private visions of becoming his hometown's savior had clouded his judgment. No one can really advance in a disintegrating situation. Learn to distinguish between imminent death and curable illness.

Yet even if the environment can improve, diminishing satisfaction may still result. Time and age may take their toll, for example. Zach R. was the Dr. Fixit for a conglomerate. He made sick operations well, and when health was restored he went on to even sicker situations. Although he became progressively better paid for his ministrations as the years rolled on, he retired early. "I guess I got sick myself after a while," he recalls now that he has headed for five years his own small electronics firm. "I felt no permanence about staying with one situation only a relatively short time — rarely more than a year — then moving on, leaving behind scores of people who hated my guts."

The false appearances discussed so far proved deceptive because of human error, misunderstanding, or the toll of time. What about a deception resulting from the outright lie? In his *Autobiography*, Benjamin Franklin describes his arduous voyage to England as a young man to take a job that he thought had been promised him. No job awaited him; he had been victimized.

Such things still happen two centuries later. To avoid that misfortune, you should examine every opportunity for promotion. If you don't know the person or persons making you an offer, try to get a line on their reputation. If you consider moving to a new employer, look him up in

Moody's, Thomas Register or other standard references. If possible, run a Dun & Bradstreet check. Beat the bushes to find someone who knows about the people and the job. Try to meet some of those people who might be working for or with you in the new position. Although it's difficult to accomplish, attempt to get a feel for the political currents that surround the new job. (See the fable of the "Blind Men and the Elephant" for more on investigating promotional opportunities.)

Finally, ask bluntly wherever possible if the new position presents any hidden reefs. Most untruths stem from omission, not commission. If you ask the right questions, few people will lie outright.

Max didn't ask the right questions in his move to New York City — so a misperception became possible. Walt practiced an even more dishonest deception on Tom in "Belling the Cat" when he conned the younger man into presenting the case for the elder's promotion. Tom lost his job for his pains.

But Walt wasn't the only con man; Tom contributed to his own deception because he naively hoped that a gain for Walt would also help him personally. When you seek a promotion, examine your own motives as well as those of the prospective employer. Do the salary and/or benefits offered seem surprisingly high? Does that influence you unduly? Are you desperate to leave your present position, and does this desperation color your judgment? Have you suffered a personality clash with someone on your present job? If so, you may be just as vulnerable to such a failing on the new job.

In short, you should do more than guard against deception from the prospective new employer. You should also watch that you don't deceive yourself.

Modern Precept for Promotion: "Deception writes 'finis' to any promotion."